RABBIT WOOL INDUSTRY IN INDIA

RABBIT WOOL INDUSTRY IN INDIA

ASHOK KUMAR
Associate Professor

S.K. Sharma R.K. Sharma Kamlesh Gupta

2004
DAYA PUBLISHING HOUSE
Delhi - 110035

ISBN 81-7035-337-8

Published by : **Daya Publishing House**
1123/74, Deva Ram Park
Tri Nagar, Delhi-110 035
Phone : 27383999
Fax : 011-27382329
e-mail : dayabooks@vsnl.com
website : www.dayabooks.com

Showroom : 4762-63/23, Ansari Road,
Darya Ganj, New Delhi-110002
Phone : 23245578, 23244987

Laser Typesetting : **P.K. Jain & Co.**

Printed at : **Chawla Offset Printers**
Delhi-110 052

PRINTED IN INDIA

ACKNOWLEDGEMENTS

The financial assistance for conducting the present work on Rabbit Wool Industry in India by Indian Council of Agricultural Research, New Delhi is thankfully acknowledged. The support given by Prof. P.K. Khosla, former Vice-Chancellor and Prof. Tej Partap, present Vice-Chancellor, Chaudhary Sarwan Kumar, Himachal Pradesh Krishi Vishvavidyalaya, Palampur is also gratefully acknowledged. Former Directors of Research Dr. Ranjodh Singh and Dr. M.P. Narang inspired us to take up the project and to accomplish its objectives within the resources of Department. We are highly grateful to both of them. We are also thankful to Dr. R.C. Thakur, the present Director of Research under whose guidance the project is completed. Thanks are also due to Dr. P.K. Sharma, the Dean, College of Agriculture for his trustful guidance in completing the project. We are also thankful to Dr. G.S. Sethi, Director of Advanced Centre of Bio-Resources and Bio-Technology for his help and guidance during the period of present investigation.

The members of research staff, Dr. Pawan Kumar, Ms. Suman Chandel, Mr. Anurag Dohroo, Mr. Adarsh Kumar and Mr. Suresh Jaswal have done a good job of data collection for which they deserve thanks and appreciation.

Time to time co-operation and help rendered by the officers of the Himachal Pradesh State Wool Federation and Government of Himachal Pradesh is duly acknowledged.

We are grateful to Dr. Parkash Mehta, former head and Dr. G.D. Vashist, present Head of the Department of Agricultural Economics for providing all necessary help and valuable suggestions during the completion of the project. We would also like to thank the Rabbit Entrepreneurs of the study area who spared their valuable time for providing information and relevant data.

Last but not the least, the secretarial help rendered by the office staff is duly acknowledged. We thank one and all whose reference has escaped us for whatever help rendered to this project. Special thanks are due to the Librarian and his staff, Ministry of Finance, New Delhi for providing assistance in data collection for the project.

Ashok Kumar
S.K. Sharma
R.K. Sharma
Kamlesh Gupta

CONTENTS

LIST OF TABLES

LIST OF FIGURES

1
INTRODUCTION

1.1 Background

The process of privatization and globalization has made every venture competitive. The macro economic reforms initiated in the country in 1991-92 have led to commercialization of agriculture keeping in view the economic viability and sustainability concepts. The effective route to development is to raise productivity of agricultural sector, which will then act as stimulus to other areas of the economy. The objectives of the government policy to meet immediate challenges of poverty, unemployment and malnutrition include full employment, economic growth, price stability, wage maintenance, reduced inequality in income distribution, regional balance, protection of the national environment, greater opportunities for women and minorities. The constraint of small holdings requires incorporation of the supplementary enterprises which not only increase productivity and income but also induces stability in the farm income. The micro-enterprises rabbits are economical because of their early maturity, prolificacy (7–8 young ones) and short gestation period (about one month). The per year collection of wool from a rabbit is 800-1000g and average meat comes to be 4 kg which is three times higher than a yield from a sheep. The rabbits require a few inputs and can be reared by workers lacking in great physical strength. Rabbitry gives an opportunity to develop 20 subsidiary industries including nursery raising wool farming, cage fabrication; feed formulation, shearing, wool collection and grading etc. The meat obtained from rabbitry is low in fat and cholesterol. It can close protein gap and raise income of rural and sub-urban people. Rabbit farming in the hilly regions of India revealed that there was a vast scope for increasing the productivity and production of Angora wool at state and national levels (Bhat, 1999).

1.2 Origin

The origin of Angora rabbit is not very definite, but it is believed to come from Abkara (Turkey) and Asia Minor. Then rabbits were brought to France and Britain by sailors and progressive breeders in the seventeenth century. It was intorduced to France at the beginning of the eighteenth century. The French farmers reared and developed Angora for wool production. In early nineteenth century, England, USA, Canada and Germany and many other countries imported rabbits and improved their productive performance by scientific breeding and management.

1.3 International Scenario

Angora production is an international industry. Angora producing countries tend not to be those with their own processing industries. The latter are not usually significant consumers of finished articles. For example, France is not a large consumer of Angora wool, yet it developed its Angora industry mainly for export. Processing industries are based in Japan, Korea, Italy, Germany and Mauritius. The main retail markets are in North America, Western Europe and Japan. There are obviously exceptions to this, for example, India, which is a significant producer, processor and consumer country. From 1950 to the present, there had been three distinct periods in the evolution of the world Angora production and consequently in the Angora trade (Rougeot and Thebault 1984, Scholaut 1985). During the first period, from 1950 to 1976, world production increased slowly from 900 tons a year to 1200 tons. It may, therefore, be considered to have been around 1000 tons a year during this period. The second period lasted 12 years, from 1976 to 1988. At the end (1988), Angora production was ten times greater than in 1976. From 1988 onwards, world production, which increased substantially since 1983, remained stable at 13,000 tons per year, but raw material price fell down from US$ 50 to 17 per kg (Ossard *et al.*, 1995).

In initial stages the focus was on producing high quality fur skins. Over a period of time FAO recognized rabbit as a meat animal. According to FAO studies, one third of the total meat production by now should come from rabbits, chicken and pigs. Accordingly the focus has seen shifted to meat production.

At present the leading rabbit meat producing counties are former Soviet Union, China, France, Italy, Spain, USA, Mexico, Cuba, Brazil, Uruguay, Republic of Korea, Japan, Ghana, Egypt, Algeria and Sudan. The rabbit skins also have good business in some parts of the world. After the slaughter of rabbits for meat, skins are harvested to obtain furs in many parts of the world, France produces about 70 million pelts. The best quality skins are tanned and then used in garments, linings, gloves etc. The skins produced in Russia and Poland are entirely used in the domestic sector. The main importers of rabbit skin from the developed countries are Republic of Korea and Philippines.

These countries completely process the skins and then re-export them to United States of America, Japan, Germany and Italy. India has been importing these skins from France to feed its fur industry. The rabbits exclusively raised for high quality furs arte Rex and Satin. Though these fur rabbits (Chinchilla, Rex, Havana, Rex) produce the valuable furs bringing as much as double the price obtained for normal furs, their production is limited one.

1.4 National Scenario

In India, rabbit industry is picking up for wool production in hilly areas (Tripathi *et al.* 1995, Jithendran, 1998). Angora rabbits were introduced during 1962 in a big way at Mohal in Kullu district of Himachal Pradesh by a private entrepreneur importing Angora rabbits from Germany. At the same time British Angoras were also reared by Mr. Butter Worth near Mcleod-Ganj, Dharamshala in Kangra district of Himachal Pradesh. The credit of introducing and popularizing Angora rabbits in India goes to ICAR through its North Temperate Regional Station of Central Sheep and Wool Research Institute (CSWRI), Garsa, Kullu. In 1970s Central Sheep and Wool Research Institute imported rabbits from USSR and UK for research and production of Angora wool, meat and fur in the country. In order to overcome the problem of reproduction and maternal care in British Angora, crossbreds were developed which were found to be widely accepted by the farmers in the Kullu Valley. The CSWRI has also introduced German Angora in 1986, which is one of the best Angora breeds today, which produces 800 to 1000 g wool per annum (Katoch, 2001).

At present the wool rabbitry is practised in Himachal Pradesh, Uttranchal, Uttar Pradesh, Jammu and Kashmir and lately in Sikkim and Arunachal Pradesh and as a broiler industry in areas of temperate and sub-tropical climate in West Bengal, Assam, Manipur, Andhra Pradesh, Tamil Nadu, Kerala and Karnataka.

1.5 State Scenario

Himachal Pradesh has emerged as a major Angora wool producing state in the country. It is estimated that out of about 30 MT per annum Angora wool production, approximately 20 MT Angora wool is produced in Himachal Pradesh. There are more than 250 units of Angora rabbits with 30,000 animals producing about 20,000 kg wool annually. These units are located mainly in Mandi, Kullu, and Kangra districts. The strength of the units varies from 10 to 1000 animals. The State Government has two Angora rabbit breeding farms, one at Kandwari near Palampur and other at Nagwain in Mandi district and having more than 1100 breedable animals at these two places (Katoch, 2001).

1.6 About the Study Area

Himachal Pradesh is located in North-India, is bounded in North by Jammu and Kashmir, east by Tibet (China), south-east by Uttranchal, south by Haryana, south-west and west by Punjab.

The area of the state is 55,673 sq km with a population of 60,77,248 with growth rate as 17.53 per cent (1991-2001). The density per square kilometer is 109. Sex-ratio (females per 1,000 males) is 970. Literacy rate is 77.13 per cent (males: 86.02 per cent; females 68.08 per cent). It has twelve districts and legislature is unicameral. The principal language and dialect are Hindi and *Pahari*. The per capita income at current prices is Rs. 15,012 against national per capita income of Rs. 16,047 in 1999-2000.

Agriculture and horticulture are the main stay of Himachal Pradesh. About 76 per cent of the total working population is engaged in these occupations. About 20 per cent of the net area sown is under irrigation. Fruits and cash crops like seed potato, ginger, vegetable seeds, apple, stone fruits, etc., are grown in the state. Wheat, maize and paddy are the major food crops. Besides apple, plum, peach and apricots are other fruit crops grown. Forests cover about 64 per cent of the area of the state.

Rock salt, slate, gypsum, limestone, dolomite and pyrites are the important minerals of Himachal Pradesh. Agro-horticulture produce, herbal resources, wool (Sheep and Angora rabbits) sericulture and electronics industries have come up in Himachal Pradesh.

1.7 Objectives of the Study

The specific objectives of the study were:

1. To study the trend in rabbit wool production in Himachal Pradesh;
2. To study the cost and profitability of wool production and to work out the optimum size alongwith break even point of rabbitry farms in Himachal Pradesh;
3. To study the market structure of rabbit wool in Himachal Pradesh;
4. To study the technological gap between existing and potential levels of rabbit wool in Himachal Pradesh;
5. To highlight the problems and constraints of rabbit wool enterprises and suggest suitable measures to overcome them.

1.8 Hypotheses

1. All categories of rabbit entrepreneurs are economically viable and earning profits.
2. Cost of production on all categories of farms is same.
3. Rabbit entrepreneurs are progressive and adopt modern technology and no technological gap exists on rabbit farms.
4. The growth in rabbit wool production in the state is significant.
5. The variability in the prices of wool is low.
6. The problems of rabbit entrepreneurs do not differ significantly on different categories of farms.

The study runs into five chapters. The importance of the study and scenario of rabbitry at different levels has been given in Chapter 1, Chapter 2 reviews the available studies on different aspects of rabbitry. Chapter-3 highlights the procedure adopted in the selection of a sample, data collection, tabulation and statistical analysis to accomplish the objectives. Chapter 4 describes the socio-economic and structural parameters of rabbit entrepreneurs Chapter 5 depicts trends in wool production. Chapter 6 computes the economics of wool production. Chapter 7 describes the marketing channels and marketing costs. Chapter 8 deals with package of practices and technological gap. Chapter 9 deseribes the problems and constraints experienced by rabbit entrepreneurs. Chapter 10 the regression analysis and Chapter 11 depicts the propects of rarbbitry for meat production Chapter-12 summaries the main findings along with suggestions and policy recommendations emerging from the study.

1.9 Usefulness of the Study

A few studies have already been carried out on some aspects of rabbitry. However, no study had been carried out which covers the entire state of Himachal Pradesh. The present study also attempts to see the past trends in wool production and prices from secondary data at the state level. An attempt has also been made to work out the break even point which suggests the minimum economically viable size of rabbitry. The problems and constraints faced at production, marketing, financial and institutional levels have also been highlighted. Based on the findings, suggestions have been made to improve the existing scenario of rabbitry. Hopefully, the study will be of immense use to economists, agricultural scientists and policy makers alike apart from its usefulness to the rabbit farmers who, if guided will be well informed about the proper use and marketing of wool.

2

REVIEW OF LITERATURE

The insight into literature gives an in-depth knowledge on the various aspects of any investigation. It shows the extent of the work done earlier on the various aspects of the problem. It also gives us the idea of lacuna in each study and designing of possible way to overcome it. It also strengthens the methodology. The Angora rabbit rearing on commercial lines is relatively a new concept. It is only about two decades back that interest in Angora rabbit rearing started and therefore, caught the attention of farm researchers.

Though, not much of the work has been undertaken on Antora rabbits so far, yet in this chapter an attempt has been made to review the available literature pertaining to the work done on various aspects of rabbit rearing in India as well as aborad. The review of various studies has been done in chronological order and categorised into four heads.

1. Prospects of rabbitry.
2. Breeding, nutrition and management.
3. Economics of rabbitry.
4. Problems, constraints and future strategy.

2.1 Prospects of Rabbitry

The plethora of studies on rabbitry established that the Angora has a great potential for providing self-employment avenues in hilly states of the country. The agro-climatic conditions of Himachal Pradesh, hilly areas of the Uttranchal and other hilly states speak of ample scope for development of Angora wool. In addition, broiler rabbit meat has relatively more proteins than beef or pork and less fat cholesterol and the rabbit skin serves as raw material for making caps, handbags, purses, jackets etc. The different studies, which speak of the prospects of rabbitry, have been given as under:

Cheeke *et al.* (1982) carried out a study on Angora wool production in USA. They found that the better type of Angoras would produce from 2 to 2.5 inches long wool in approximately 11 weeks. This represented 12 to 16 ounces of wool. They further revealed that when properly balanced rations were fed 100 pounds of feed was required, on an average, to produce one pound of wool.

Schlolaut (1985) conducted a study on production performance of rabbits in Germany. He observed that the average period utilization of animals for wool production was 3 to 4 years and the highest performances were obtained at an age of 10 to 14 months. He also reported that the wool yield could be increased by reducing the shearing interval but feed and labour costs were also raised. He emphasized on separate rearing of breeding and wool producing rabbits for better results.

Makhohlane (1987) studied rabbit as a production animal in South Africa. He highlighted the potential economic benefits and feasibility of increased rabbit farming in South African countries. The author found that the combination of a high reproductive rate, low energy requirement per kilogram of live-weight gain and high wool price made rabbit production a potentially lucrative activity.

Rai *et al.* (1987) made a study on opening of a rabbitry at Garsa in Kullu valley of Himachal Pradesh. They found that the optimum environmental temperature for rabbits was 15–25°C. The temperature beyound 25°C resulted in uneasiness and poor production, if accompanied with direct sun-light resulted in sunstrokes also. The authors suggested that the meat rabbits could be successfully reared in slightly higher temperature *i.e.*, 30–35°C, but their fur quality deteriorated whereas, in case of Angora rabbits, the wool growth and quality were affected.

Phull *et al.* (1989) carried out a study on rabbit rearing for wool in Kangra districts of Himachal Pradesh. They observed that a rabbitry unit of 10 females and 2 males could generate the net returns equal to Rs. 57,148 after two years. They also worked out the benefit cost ratio which came out to be 1.62 : 1.00.

Singh (1990) conducted a study on rabbit rearing at Indian Veterinary Research Institute, Regional Station, Palampur in Himachal Pradesh. He concluded that Angora rabbits have a brighter future in Himachal Pradesh and Angora rabbit was the only breed of rabbits from which wool for spinning could be obtained. The author also reported that a mature Angora rabbit weighed 2.5 to 4.0 kg produced 1200 g of wool per annum. Production of wool was dependent upon the strain, dietary and environmental factors.

Sudheer *et al.* (1995) studied the scope and feasibility of rabbit farming. According to them the food babits of Indians were changing and the demand for meat was day by day increasing in the country. Our conventional meat producers like cattle, goats, sheep, pigs and poultry would not be able to meet this demand. Rabbit, which has a great potential as a meat producer is one of the alternatives. They were highly prolific and quick growing. Apart from meat rabbit wool and pellets were also of great economic value. Rabbit rearing did not require huge investment like other livestock enterprises. Rabbit husbandry could generate great employment potential for hundreds of jobless youth and women folk of the country. They also studied the processing of rabbit skin. According to them by processing the skin of rabbit we would get superior quality leather of high economic value which could be used for making variety of leather goods such as bags, gloves hats, shoes etc.

Tripathi (1997) studied the production and marketing of Angora wool products in Uttar Pradesh hills and found that Angora wool products had a great potential to generate additional income and employment in the hills of Uttar Pradesh. The scale of business, particularly in processing and making the finished products, needed to be increased so that the efficient and modern processing chines and equipments would be introduced in the enterprises which would certainly reduce per unit cost of the processing. For increasing the share of producer and wholesaler and retailer must be rationalized through making and execution of effective marketing regulations for commission rates in angora products. Establishment of Angora wool producer and processor co-operative societies in and around the area could be helpful in increasing the bargaining power of the producer during marketing process.

Sharma, A.K.(1998) studied the untapped potential of rabbitry in Himachal Pradesh and revealed that there was a need to learn a lesson from countries like France, Germany, Czechoslovakia, USA and UK. China at present was producing 1.20 lakh tonnes of meat and 6.000 tonnes of Angora wool per year earning a hard currency of about $ 2 billion per year by export. In Himachal Pradesh the industry was suffering because of lowering down of prices over the years due to the imported wool which was available at a cheaper rate. The people needed awareness that the average collection of wool from a rabbit is 1 kg and average meat comes to be 4 kg which was three times higher than yield from sheep.

Saxena *et al.* (1998) conducted a pilot study revealed that rabbit farming was a profitable enterprise which not only augments income by sale of wool (Angora) and meat but also gives an opportunity to raise the social status of farmers. The overall average wool yield per adult rabbit per shearing was of the order of 131 g, whereas, that of young stock in the age of 5–6 months irrespective of sex was of the order of 93 g per shearing only.

Sharma (2000) revealed that rabbitry was a hidden treasure and not being explored to the desired extent. The meat obtained from rabbits was safe because of low fat and cholesterol levels. Therefore, it gave an edge over chicken, mutton and pork. Studies have revealed that Globally; more than 90 per cent of the rabbit production came from little farms with only a few does. In Himachal Pradesh with the introduction of German Angora in 1986, the wool rabbitry started flourishing and wool prices were as high as Rs. 1000 per kg. When the rabbitry profession was in a few hands, they sold castrated bucks for the purpose of wool production and breeding remained in their own hands. However, the rabbitry being such a lucrative profession could not yield desired results as the rabbit entrepreneurs were in great distress.

Katoch (2001) revealed that Angora had a great potential for providing self employment avenues in hilly area of the country. The agro-climatic conditions of Himachal Pradesh, hilly areas of the Uttar Pradesh and other hilly states spoke of ample scope for development of Angora fur. In addition, broiler rabbit meat had relatively more proteins than beef or pork and had less fat, cholesterol and the rabbit skins served as raw material for making caps, handbags, purses, jackets etc. However, Himachal Pradesh was the largest Angora wool producing state in the country. Rabbitry was taken-up by about 250 private entrepreneurs.

Kishore (2001) revealed that a good German Angora rabbit of 4 kg live weight would yield, on an average, 200 g of quality wool per kg body weight per year. This was about four times higher than a Merino Sheep (reared in India) weighing 40 kg and producing, on an average 3 kg, greasy fleece per annum thus representing 75 g of wool produced per kg of body weight. Further more whereas Angora wool did not need scouring, the Merino wool scouring loss is about 50 per cent meaning thereby that Angora rabbit produced 5–6 times more wool per unit live weight than the Merino Sheep. The generation interval was small (gestation period about one month), useful by-products like meat, fur skins and manure.

2.2. Breeding, Nutrition and Management

In rabbitry, breeding aspect is important as inbreeding resulted into high mortality, poor yield and low returns. Equally important are nutrition and management aspects for successful performance of rabbitry. Some of the studies on breeding, nutrition and management aspects were reviewed hereunder as:

Sawal *et al.* (1991) studied feed related toxic factors in rabbit farming. Their study was based on anti-nutritional factors which were widespread in animals feeds. Most feeds had nore than one anti-nutritional factors and the level at which these were present was important. Every living being had its own detoxification mechanisms which inactivated these factor only up to a certain level, beyond which adverse effects appeared. They also studied the factor affecting protein metabolism.

Kumar *et al.* (1992) studied the different breeds of Angora rabbits and found that for efficient breeding and growth, a temperature range of 10–20°C was required in rabbit shed. The ideal humidity for indoor rabbits should be 60–65 per cent. The rabbit house should also be well drained, should not be situated at the bottom of a deep valley nor totally enclosed with trees. The balance feed for rabbits should have 16–18 per cent crude protein,

10–14 per cent crude fibre, 2–5 per cent total fats, 2200–2500 K Cal/kg metabolizable energy with a total digestibility of 65–70 per cent.

Singh (1996) made a study on feeding of rabbits and revealed that feed accounted for more than 70 per cent of the total cost of production. He suggested that a diet having 12–15 per cent crude fibre during growth, pregnancy and lactation and about 14 per cent for maintenance was adequate for rabbits. He further recommended that the feed ingredients for rabbits should be coarsely ground because the finely ground material stayed in the hindgut for a longer period and allowed growth of pathogenic bacteria which caused enterities.

Takkar (1997) studied the reproductive management of rabbits and found that one female rabbit (doe) on an average could produce 6-8 kits and 4-6 litters in a year. Thus, a doe could produce 24-18 kits in a year depending on their overall management. He revealed that rabbits should be procured from reputed breeding farm between 3 and 4 months of age in the ratio of 3 female : 1 male and should be kept in cages measuring 61 cm x 61 cm x 46 cm for male and 61 cm x 46 cm x 46 cm for female in the sheds and may be in one, two or three tier system.

Jithendran (1998) studied rabbit production in sub-Himalayan region and revealed that rabbits easily adapted to varying climatic conditions. Rabbits lacked functional sweat glands which caused thermoregulatory problem during hot and humid climate. The optimum temperature and relative humidity for rabbit rearing was 15-20^{0}C and 60-70 per cent respectively. He observed the concentrate feed was to be provided 60-70 g per adult and 150 g for female with kids. Rabbits consumed most of their feed 60–70 per cent at night before dawn. They preferred pelleted food. Rabbits liked tree leaves such as biul (*Grewia optiva* and *Grewia robusta*), mulberry (*Morus alba*), bamboo (*Dendrocalamus strictus*) etc. They also liked barseem and Lucerne.

Bhat (1999) made a study in different districts of Himachal Pradesh in the year of 1999. He studied about Angora rabbit farming in the hilly regions of India. He observed rabbit farming for wool and meat production had become increasingly popular in our country during the last two decades and a number of rabbitry units have been set up in the temperate and sub-tropically hilly regions of Himachal Pradesh, Jammu and Kashmir, Uttar Pradesh north eastern sates and southern states like Tamil Nadu, Kerala and Karnataka. In Himachal Pradesh rabbit farming started with the rearing of both meat and fur breeds. He also observed that there were number of countries where rabbits farming centers were found like in China, Japan, Argentina and Republic of Korea. The Chinese production was highest at over 6000 tonnes in year out of total production of 8000 tonnes. Wool production is only 40 tonnes out of which Himachal Pradesh accounted for more than half (24 tonnes). He also observed that there were number of advantages in rearing Angora rabbit on a commercial scale. Angora rabbits were suited to backyard and small scale production as well as large-scale commercial production. These animals needed relatively inexpensive housing, are lighly adaptable and could be raised under a wide variety of housing systems. He studied the distinctive features of angora rabbit wool. He also observed that due to their feeding habits, Angora rabbits could be easily maintained on high forage, low grain diet which is unsuited for human consumption. Moreover as compared to other livestock, they required low level of nutrients and energy. Thus rabbit meat and wool could be produced on kitchen waste on toxic weeds, locally available leaves and agricultural and industrial byproducts.

Guleria (2001) described the characteristics of successful entrepreneurs in rabbit farming and revealed that entrepreneurship referred to identifying ideas, products and services, mobilizing resources, organising production, services and finally marketing them covering the risk with constant strive for growth and excellence. The characteristics of successful entrepreneurs were: self-confidence of high level, long-term involvement, money as a measure, persistent problem solving, goal setting, moderate risk taking, dealing with failure, use of feedback, taking initiative and seeking personal responsibility, use of resources, tolerance of ambiguity and uncertainty.

Katoch (2001) revealed that for purchasing breeding stock, the important points to be considered were: it was always desirable to obtain stock from number of different sources to create genetic diversity, to begin with two bucks and 5 to 10 does were enough, purchase mature stock or junior animals when they were weaned, source of rabbitry should be free from diseases and when breeding stock was purchased from a small herd, it was always better to buy bucks from different sources than the does, so as to facilitate maximum genetic diversity. He further studied the different breeding systems like inbreeding, line breeding, out breeding and cross breeding. The best breeding system depended upon, quality of the stock, purpose of the producer (meat production or wool production) and genetic variability in animals.

Katoch (2001) studied the economical feeding of commercial rabbits and also suggested well-balanced and economical general purpose rabbit feeds and revealed that the size of the pellets was an important consideration. The growing stock should be fed pellets of approximately 2 mm diameter. The length of the pellets should preferably be adjusted to 4-6 mm. When the kits were housed along with the doe, the pellet size should preferable be 3 mm diameter and 4-6 mm in length to facilitate proper intakes by both types of stock. The pellets should be fairly hard, because these animals had a tendency to cut the bits of the pellets before inpestion. Since the feed cost was the major item of expenditure in the commercial rabbit rearing, this component should preferably be barest minimum.

Sood (2001) studied the reproduction in rabbits. He revealed that bucks and does mature at the same age. In general, does generally reached puberty when they had grown to 70–75 per cent of their mature weight. It is usually preferable to wait until they reached 80 per cent of their mature weight. Factors influencing puberty and sexual maturity were breed and strains of a breed. The small breeds reached breeding age at about 5 months, while the larger meat producing breed may take more time. The oestrous cycle to be of 16–19 days during which a doe remained receptive for 12–15 days. Rabbits could be bred at all seasons of the year. A receptive doe had an arched back, raised hind quarter and the most pertinent sign of raised tail lifted towards. The aggressive behaviour at the time of mating or crouching to the corner of the cage suggested a non-receptive phase.

Thakur (2001) studied the effect of environmental conditions on rabbit production and found that rabbits suffered more from heat than from cold, so more attention should be given to herd during periods of high temperatures. High temperature also impaired the reproductive performance and feed intake of rabbits. The rabbits were much more sensitive to air quality (relative humidity, concentration of noxious gases and movement of air) than to temperature. So proper ventilation of the rabbitry was also essential. Direct light should be avoided. For a continual production of young throughout the year, constant duration of light from 12–16 hours per day was, therefore, recommended. Angora rabbits for wool production should be given 16–9 hour decreasing duration of lighting in the course of the shearing interval. Two 40 watt tubes per 10 square metre or 100 square feet would provide illumination satisfactorily.

2.3 Economics of Rabbitry

The economics of wool production is very important as far as success of this industry is concerned. The various studies available on economics of wool production have been reviewed and presented in chronological order in the proceeding paragraphs.

Lall *et al.* (1984) worked out economics of Angora rabbit husbandry for small self-employed farmers, operating a small animal unit for wool, at Palampur. Based on their study the fixed cost components included the construction of shed, purchase of animals, cages and small implements. The variable costs consisted of depreciation on rabbits and cages, insurance of animals, charges on water and electricity and expenditure incurred on feed, medicines and veterinary services etc. The returns included the value of wool sold and value of manure. The annual profit per rabbit was calculated to be 44 per cent of the capital outlay. They further found that the margin of profit was much higher if the farmer did not construct a new shed for housing of animals. The annual profit at 44 per cent of the total outlay was substantially over the commercial rate of interest.

Zimmerman *et al.* (1985) undertook a study in Germany to provide a guidance for an objective evaluation of rabbit production from an economic point of view. They found that the same principles were helpful in calculating the gross margin for wool as well as for meat production, however, difference was noticed in the treatment of animal losses. They revealed that due to frequent shearing, losses did not play a role in the proportional expenditures and could, therefore, be disregarded and applied them to the animal. Here the average value of the purchase and slaughter price should be estimated. They further pointed out that the factors of greatest economic importance were wool yield, wool price and feed requirement and even a slight alteration in these components had a substantial effect on the success of the project. Therefore, any measures taken should primarily be aimed at the improvement of these factors.

Lebas *et al.* (1986) performed a study on economic management of a rabbitry in Rome. Their study revealed that the operating costs which could vary with the production system accounted for a rabbit farm with 100 breeding does came out to be 70 per cent of the total cost of production. Feed accounted for 65 per cent of the total outlay. The depreciation of building and equipment together with financial charges accounted for more than 25 per cent of the total cost. Based on these cost components, they concluded that maintenance of feed efficiency was the most important factor on a rabbit farm for achieving higher profits.

Martineze (1987) made a study on technical and economic results of rabbit production in Spain. The author analysed various costs returns involved in the rabbit production. He compared the results of the leading producers with those of average producers in order to identify the causes of differences. He found that the major factors responsible for the differences were the shortening of reproductive cycle to increase births and reduction of mortality by improving conditions and an increase in the number of young weaned by does. He observed that the leading producers had lower feed cost on their farms. He further advocated that in order to regulate supply throughout the year, the number of rabbits added to the reproductive stock was required to be increased at mid year and un-productive does culled. Production indices were highest in the smallest units, this might be the result of better reproduction management and fewer health problems.

Phull *et al.* (1989) carried out a study on rabbit rearing for wool in Kangra district of Himachal Pradesh. They observed that a rabbitry limit of 10 females and 2 males could generate the net returns equal to Rs. 57.148 after two years. They also worked out the benefit cost ratio which came out to be 1.52 : 1.00.

Manuja (1990) worked out the economics of Angora rabbit farming at Agriculture University, Palampur. He revealed that for a unit size of 10 females and 2 males, at the time of establishment, the benefit-cost ratio at the end of first year was 1.65 : 1.00.

Sharma *et al.* in 1998 studied economic viability, technological gap, problems and future strategy to enhance export of rabbit wool in Kangra district of Himachal Pradesh. They studied that rabbitry opened new vistas of self-employment to educated youth. They observed that wool rabbits were more profitable than meat rabbits. The benefit cost ratio was estimated to be 1.51:1 in meat rabbits and 2.1:1 in wool rabbits. The study of technological gap existed for the use of roughage, followed by cage size. However, there was over use of medicines and labour input on rabbit farms. The study of problem and constraints revealed that the availability of fresh blood, remunerative prices and sufficiency of market system had been reported by 100 per cent of the farmers. They concluded that the supply of quality feed and other inputs along with exotic germplasm for crossbreeding would go a long way to improve the status of rabbit farmers.

Sharma and Sharma (2001) studied the economic viability of wool rabbits on different size of farms in Kullu and Mandi districts and revealed that the cost of production and size of farm had negative correlation. However, the gross returns and size of farm were positively correlated. The net profitability of rabbit rearing over total cost revealed that the farmers were incurring losses except the large farms of Mandi district. The net profitability over variable cost revealed that large farms in Kullu district and medium and large farms in Mandi district were earning a marginal profits.

2.4 Problems, Constraints and Future Strategy

Rabbit production requires technical knowledge for its success. The studies showing problems and constraints in rabbit production along with suggestions given through various studies have been reviewed as below:

Cheeke *et al.* (1982) pointed out that frequent visitors in a commercial rabbitry be avoided, as they might bring disease organisms with them. They suggested that installations of a viewing window at one end of the building may reduce the stress on rabbits caused due to noise and prevent the rabbitry from infection.

James *et al.* (1986) performed a study on the effect of waste water in rabbitries at the center for Small Farm Research, Southern University, Baton Rouge. They revealed that the reduction of waste water in a rabbitry was desirable because the water increased the humidity in the building and was, thus, a pre-disposing factor to disease. They also found that the installation of gutters under the drinkers reduced the problem with wet floors and also the moisture problem in the building.

Singh *et al.* (1987) made a study on care of rabbits in Kullu Valley of Himachal Pradesh. Their study revealed that the castrated male rabbits produced about 20 per cent more wool than entire ones. They further suggested that whenever there were a large number of males in the rabbitry and there was no way to dispose off those surplus males, they might be castrated.

Gulyani *et al.* (1990) performed a study on structure of rabbitry in Kullu Valley of Himachal Pradesh. They found that top quality of Angora wool was produced from animals at the age of nine months and above. The wool yield remained fairly high till 2 to 3 years and then started declining. Based on the observations they advised to keep an animal as long as it was economically viable. They also reported that maintaining a predominantly adult population in a rabbitry reduced the mortality rate over the years. They emphasized the need for castrating the surplus males as it not only shortened the difference in wool yield between the male and female rabbit, but also reduced the cost of raising.

Jithendran (1991) studied the different constraints faced by the farmers in rabbit rearing and revealed that compared to other farm livestock and poultry, rabbit production was more demanding of technical knowledge and care. Due to the less production performance at high temperature rabbit production was less suitable for hot humid tropics. Feed was expensive and is the major cost of production. Lack of proper marketing of rabbit meat, fur and wool were major constraint faced by the farmers.

Phull (1991) suggested that for the successful rabbitry steps should be taken to establish organized wool markets in the major rabbitry pockets in the state. The credit should also be made available. The government should take steps to provide breeding stock at subsidized rate through government farms. One feed plant could be set-up for a cluster of farmers to cater to the needs of various rabbit farmers. More training courses should be organized and farmers should form small co-operatives for the sale of rabbit products. Such an institution could also extend credit or make arrangements for the supply of various inputs required in a rabbitry.

Sharma (1991) studied the constraints in population of rabbit farming and categorised the constraints as social, psychological, situational, operational and institutional problems. He revealed that transfer of science technology was greatly affected and hampered by the social and psychological constraints. Among operational problems the availability of fresh blood, recurrence of aflatoxins, rise in feed prices were the main constraints. In marketing problems unremunerative prices of wool, inefficient marketing system, monopoly of purchases, inappropriate grading and import of Angora yarn, made Angora farming an economical.

Bhat (1999) studied Angora rabbit farming in hilly areas and revealed that there was a vast scope for increasing the productivity and production of Angora wool at state and national levels. The author also highlighted the distinctive features of Angora rabbit wool and constraints in Angora rabbit farming. Among the major recommendations he made for successful farming of Angora rabbits were that the breeding stock should be young and procured from a well-managed rabbitry with least disease problems. The beginners should preferably start with two bucks and ten does. The shearing should be avoided in the cold months of December and January. Animal performance and financial records should be maintained properly. Among major constraints are the slumps in wool prices, import of Angora yarn resulting in glut in the market, rise in feed prices, continued disease problems, improper training of farmers and lack of practical experience of trainer were reported. He stressed on imparting education to rabbit entrepreneurs.

Sharma *et al.* (2001) studied the reasons of recession is rabbit industry and revealed that slashing down of import duty had adversely affected the domestic industry. The other reasons included rise in feed prices, incidence of food poisoning, lack of quality wool processing plants, lack of technical knowledge, lack of market and inbreeding among animal had reduced the quality and quantity of rabbit wool. The feed plants and processing of rabbit wool should be installed locally on co-operative basis. Package of practices on rabbitry should be made available and rabbitry for meat should be encouraged.

The review of available studies on prospects, breeding, nutrition, management, economic aspect, problems of rabbit entrepreneurs and future strategy revealed that rabbit farming it takenup on scientific lines can provide self employment avenues and greater profits. The problem of non-availability of fresh blood and low prices of the wool were major constraints. The installation of feed plants and wool processing units can go a long way in boosting the rabbit industry.

3

METHODOLOGY

A scientific methodology adopted for the study leads to reliable findings. The review of the available studies and their methodology gives an idea for developing better techniques to accomplish objectives of the investigation. The present chapter describes the locale of the study, sampling design and analytical tools employed to meet the objectives of the study.

3.1 Locale of the Study

The present study pertains to whole of Himachal Pradesh. The entire Himachal Pradesh has been divided into four agro-climatic zones. Out of four zones, three agro-climatic zones offer an opportunity for developing wool rabbitry. However, meat rabbits have wider adaptability and can be taken-up in all the four zones of Himachal Pradesh. The study zones are; low hills subtropical, mid-hills sub humid, high hills temperate wet and high hills temperate dry. The demarcation of the zones has been done by the experts from Indian Council of Agricultural Research (I.C.A.R.), Chaudhary Sarwan Kumar Himachal Pradesh Krishi Vishvavidyalaya, Palampur (H.P.) and the State Directorate of Agriculture, depending upon the physical and climatic conditions.

3.2 Salient Features of Different Zones

The salient features of agro-climatic zones of Himachal Pradesh have been depicted in Table 3.1.

The annual rainfall in the state varies from 247.2 cm in certain parts of Kangra district to only 12.4 cm in the district of Lahaul and Spiti and Kinnaur and Pangi sub-division of Chamba district. The high hill temperate dry zone with very low rainfall remains covered

TABLE 3.1: **Salient features of agro-climatic zones of Himachal Pradesh**

S. No.	*Particulars*	*Zone-I*	*Zone-II*	*Zone-III*	*Zone-IV*
1.	Total Geographical Area ('000 ha)	913.20 (16.24)	1183.20 (21.25)	1280.90 (23.01)	2190.00 (39.34)
2.	Elevation (metres)	Below 650 m.s.1.	650–1800 m.s.1.	1800–2200 m.s.1.	2200 m.s.1. and
3.	Rainfall (mm)	1000	1500–3000	1000	250
4.	Total Cropped Area ('000 ha)	355.10 (38.00)	383.40 (41.04)	171.80 (18.39)	24.00 (2.57)
5.	Gross Irrigated Area ('000 ha)	58.95 (39.52)	67.09 (44.97)	13.40 (8.98)	9.74 (6.53)
6.	Per cent Irrigated Area to total cultivated area	16.60	17.50	7.80	40.60
7.	Per cent Cropped Area of total geographical area	32.43	32.40	13.41	1.10

Source: National Agril. Research Project Report of Himachal Pradesh, ICAR, New Delhi, 1982.

with snow usually from November to April. About 70 to 80 per cent of the total precipitation is received during the monsoon season and the remainder in the winter season, with April, May, October and November usually being the dry months. Relative humidity varies from 47.0 to 90.5 per cent in different months.

3.2.1 Sub-mountain and low-hills sub-tropical zone (Zone-I)

This zone comprises the areas adjoining Punjab and Haryana states. Table 3.1 and Table 3.2 present the salient features and coverage in different zones of the state. The zone-1 lies below 650 m above the mean sea level (m.s.l.) and accounts for 16.24 per cent of total geographical area of the state. This zone covers the districts of Una, Hamirpur and Bilaspur and parts of Sirmaur, Kangra, Solan and Chamba districts. The rainfall is 1000 mm per annum. Most of the rainfall is received during monsoon season. It accounts for about 38 per cent of the total cropped area and 40 per cent of the total irrigated area of the state. The major sources of irrigation are wells and tube-wells.

TABLE 3.2: District-wise coverage in different zones of Himachal Pradesh

Zones	Special Name	Coverage
Zone-I	Sub-mountain low hills sub-tropical	Una, Bilaspur, Hamirpur districts and parts of Sirmaur, Kangra, Solan and Chamba districts.
Zone-II Kangra	Mid-hills sub-humid	Palampur and Kangra tehsils of district. Rampur tehsil of Shimla and parts of Mandi, Solan, Kullu, Chamba and Sirmaur districts.
Zone-III	High-hills temperate wet	Shimla (except Rampur tehsil) parts of Kullu, Solan, Chamba, Mandi, Kangra and Sirmaur districts.
Zone-IV	High-hills Temperate dry	Kinnaur, Lahaul-Spiti districts and parts of Chamba district.

Source: National Agril. Research Project Report of Himachal Pradesh, ICAR, New Delhi, 1982.

The study of the cropping pattern in the zone-I revealed that it is dominated by foodgrains, especially cereals, which cover 85 per cent of the total area of the zone. The main crop of *kharif* is maize and that of *rabi* is wheat covering an area of 33.91 and 40.83 per cent of the total cropped area, respectively. Paddy and pulses account for 9.80 and 11.91 per cent of the area, respectively. The area under oilseeds is only 2.36 per cent. The fruits, which cover about 3 per cent of the cropped area, include citrus and other subtropical fruits like litchi, mango, guava etc. In general, traditional farming is followed by majority of the farmers and there exists tremendous potential for sub-tropical fruits and vegetable farming.

3.2.2 Mid-hills sub-humid zone (Zone-II)

The zone comprises the area ranging from 650 to 1800 m above mean sea level. This zone accounts for 21.25 per cent of the total geographical area of the state. The zone covers major parts of Mandi and Solan districts and parts of Kangra, Shimla, Kullu, Chamba and Sirmaur districts. The rainfall ranges from 1500 to 3000 mm per annum. The high rainfall area of Dharamshala and Palampur also lies in this zone. The principal crops of the zone are maize and wheat accounting for 24.13 and 27.54 per cent of the total cropped area in the zone. As a result of availability of more irrigation water in this zone, paddy has emerged as an important *kharif* crop of the zone accounting for 13.98 per cent of the total cultivated area. In this zone, the area under foodgrains is about 77 per cent of the total cropped area. The zone is also famous for the production of various off-season vegetable crops, vegetable crop seeds especially cauliflower and rabbitry.

3.2.3 High-hills temperate-wet zone (Zone-Ill)

This zone consists of high hills and mountain areas of the state. The zone includes major parts of Shimla and Kullu districts and parts of Solan, Mandi, Chamba, Kangra and Sirmaur districts with an altitude of 1800–2200 m above mean sea level. This zone accounts for 23.01 per cent of the total geographical area of the state. In this zone about 90 per cent area is under pastures and forests. The *kuhls* and storage, tanks are the only source of irrigation in the zone. The foodgrains cover about 91 per cent of the total cropped area. The seed potato is most important cash crop of the zone and accounts for about 5 per cent of the cropped area. This zone is also known as the fruit-bowl of Himachal Pradesh especially, apple. This zone alone accounts for more than 60 per cent of the total area under apple in the state.

3.2.4 High-hills temperate-dry zone (Zone-IV)

This zone covers the tribal areas of Himachal Pradesh. The zone covers the districts of Kinnaur and Lahaul-Spiti and parts of Chamba district with altitude of more than 2200 m above mean sea level–rainfall is very low which is about 250 mm per annum and temperature remains low almost throughout the year. Most of the area of this zone is under snow clad and rocky cold desert mountains. The zone accounts only for 2.6 per cent of the total cropped area of the state and only about 1 per cent of the total geographical area of zone. The *Kuhls* are the main source of irrigation. Barley and wheat are the important foodgrains grown in the area.

The cultivators of this zone have started growing high value rare crops like *kuth*, hops, black cumin, saffron etc. This zone is also suitable for raising sheep and goats which is also the mainstay of most of the tribal people of this zone.

The different agro-climatic zones of Himachal Pradesh along with area of coverage have been shown in Fig 3.1.

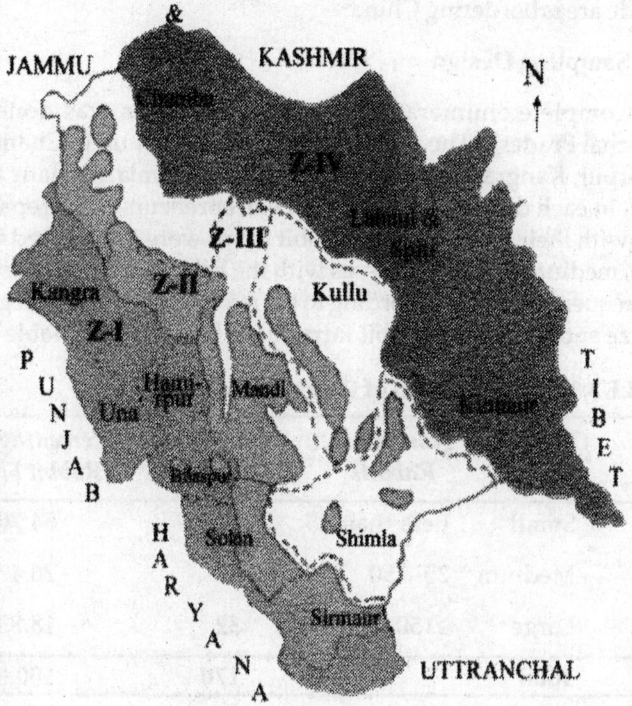

FIG.1 AGRO-CLIMATIC ZONES OF HIMACHAL PRADESH

FIG. 3.1 : Agro-climatic zones of Himachal Pradesh

3.2.5 Overall view of agro-climatic conditions in Himachal Pradesh

The geographical boundaries of Himachal Pradesh extend over the Himalayas varying in altitude from 300–6500 metres above mean sea level. The climatic conditions in the state thus vary from subtropical in lower altitude areas adjoining the plains of Punjab. Haryana and Uttar Pradesh to alpine type in the higher latitude areas bordering China.

3.3 Sampling Design

Complete enumeration of the rabbit farms was done in Himachal Pradesh. The rabbitry for wool is taken-up in Chamba, Hamirpur, Kangra, Kinnaur, Kullu, Mandi, Shimla, Sirmaur and Solan. In each district a list of rabbit entrepreneurs was prepared alongwith their flock size. The rabbit farms were categorised into small, medium and large classes with the help of cumulative cube root frequency method according to the flock size. For each category the size and number of rabbit farms have been given in Table 3.3.

TABLE 3.3 : Classification of the rabbit farms

S. No.	*Category*	*Number of Rabbits*	*Number of Rabbit Farms*	*Percentage of Rabbit Farm*
1.	Small	Less than 25	93	54.70
2.	Medium	25–150	45	26.47
3	Large	≥150	32	18.83
	Total		**170**	**100.00**

Source: Primary data from the rabbit entrepreneurs.

3.3.1 Selection of districts

Rabbitry for wool is taken-up in all districts except Una, Bilaspur and Lahaul and Spiti, where the climatic conditions are not congenial. Chamba, Hamirpur, Kangra, Kinnaur, Kullu, Mandi, Shimla and Solan districts were chosen for the study.

3.3.2 Selection of rabbit farms

Complete enumeration of rabbit farms in all the selected districts was done. The list of rabbit entrepreneurs in each district was obtained with the help of officials of the Development Blocks, progressive rabbit entrepreneurs, traders, concerned officials of government etc. The number of rabbit entrepreneurs in different categories in each district has been given in Table 3.4

TABLE 3.4 : Distribution of rabbit entrepreneurs in selected districts of HimachalPradesh

S. No.	Districts	Size of Farm			
		Small	Medium	Large	Total
1.	Chamba	19	–	–	19
2.	Hamirpur	–	–	05	05
3.	Kangra	07	07	02	16
4.	Kinnaur	05	–	–	05
5.	Kullu	04	14	08	26
6.	Mandi	01	18	22	41
7.	Shimla	03	–	–	03
8.	Solan	54	01	–	55
	Total	**93**	**40**	**37**	**170**

Source: Primary data from the rabbit entrepreneurs.

3.4 Time Dimension of Study

The study pertains to three agricultural years viz; 1997-98, 1998-1999 and 1999-2000.

3.5 Collection of data

The study is based on primary as well as secondary data. The primary data were collected on well-designed pre-tested schedule by personal interview method, whereas, the secondary data were collected from various offices and publications.

3.5.1. Primary data

The primary data were collected from rabbit entrepreneurs, wool traders, scientists, veterinary officers and officials of the Himachal Pradesh State Wool Federation on the following aspects:

- Demographic structure such as sex, age, education and type and composition of family;
- Inventory of land and rabbits;
- Inventory of rabbitry sheds;
- Composition and strength of rabbit units;
- Procurement of breeding stock;
- Mortality in rabbitry;
- Quantity of feed;
- Use of medicines and other material inputs;
- Utilisation of labour for different operations;
- Investment on cages, feeders, waterers, equipments, machinery and other items related to rabbitry;
- Various items of other fixed investment and the sources of finance;
- Sale and purchase of breeding and other stock;
- Interval in wool shearing;
- Quantity and type of fodder fed to rabbits;
- Disposal and prices of rabbit wool;
- Disposal of excreta as a manure;
- Marketing channels;
- Marketing costs and margins;
- Processing cost of rabbit wool;
- Saleable products from rabbit wool;
- Input-output prices;
- Borrowings of rabbit entrepreneurs;
- Sources of technical guidance;
- Training on rabbitry;
- Total income of rabbit entrepreneurs from different sources;
- Problems and constraints faced by rabbit entrepreneurs.

3.5.2 Secondary data

The following secondary data were collected from various sources :

1. The Office of the Block Development Officers:
   - List of villages taking-up rabbitry;
   - List of rabbit entrepreneurs in each village.
2. Government Rabbit Farm, Kandwari (Kangra):
   - List of rabbit farmers to whom breeding rabbits were distributed in the study area;
   - Feeding schedule and different strains of wool rabbits.
3. Central Sheep and Wool Research and Training Centre, Garsa (Kullu):
   - Various aspects of on-going research and list of rabbit entrepreneurs to whom rabbits were distributed.
4. Chaudhary Sarwan Kumar Himachal Pradesh Krishi Vishvavidyalaya, Palampur:
   - Recommended package of practices;
   - Technical guidance at every stage of project handling.
5. Department of Animal Husbandry, Government of Himachal Pradesh:
   - Total production of wool in the state.
6. H.P. State Wool Federation, Shimla:
   - Distribution of rabbitry in different districts and population of rabbits;
   - Procurement and price of rabbit wool over time;
   - Suggestions for promoting rabbitry.
7. Feed merchants at different locations:
   - Prices of feed;
   - List of rabbit farmers.
8. Medical Stores:
   - Prices of medicines used in rabbit rearing.

9. Statistical outline of Himachal Pradesh, 1998:
   - Data of different districts etc.
10. Ministry of Finance, New Delhi:
    - Customs duty on rabbit wool in different years.

The help was also sought from Indian Agricultural Statistical Research Institute, New Delhi for techniques and methods for data analysis. The methodologies used were discussed with the economists in the Division of Agricultural Economics at Indian Agricultural Research Institute, New Delhi.

3.6 The Analytical Framework

The primary and secondary data collected during the three years were checked, scrutinized, categorised, coded, tabulated, analysed, compiled and presented systematically. To achieve the specified objectives the simple mathematical and statistical tools were employed.

3.6.1 Mathematical analysis

The simple tables were prepared to present the socio-economic aspects of rabbit entrepreneurs. The following parameters were computed:

- Agewise and castewise distribution of rabbit entrepreneurs
- Family composition
- Educational status of rabbit entrepreneurs
- Occupational distribution of households
- Distribution of land and livestock
- Total household income
- Acquisition of rabbits by rabbit entrepreneurs
- Comparative picture of establishment of rabbit farms in different districts of Himachal Pradesh
- Investment on tools, equipment and machinery pertaining to rabbit keeping
- Production of rabbit wool and its utilization
- Borrowings on rabbit farms

3.6.2 Cost and return analysis

The cost and return analysis has been done on 100 animal basis. The various components of the costs are as follow:

3.6.2.1 Depreciation of fixed assets

The annual depreciation of fixed assets like farm buildings, electric fittings and water supply installations was worked out by assuming the economic life of these assets. Similarly the depreciation charges of animals were calculated by assuming their economic life as three years. The depreciation of various equipments like cages, kindling boxes, feeders, waterers etc., was estimated at the rate of 10 per cent.

3.6.2.2 Interest on fixed assets

Interest on fixed assets was charged at the rate of 12 per cent per annum which is concessional rate of interest charged by commercial banks for setting up of rabbitry units.

3.6.2.3 Variable cost

The variable cost in a rabbitry includes the cost of feed, roughages, wages of labour, cleaning of shed, shearing, expenditure on medicines, electricity, watering, expenditure on disinfectants etc.

3.6.2.3.1 Feed cost

The feed cost was obtained by multiplying the quantity of feed fed and the rate of its purchase. For home grown feeds the quantities fed were evaluated in monetary terms taking into consideration the nearest market value.

3.6.2.3.2 Labour cost

Total labour cost was the sum of paid labour and unpaid labour. The actual amount paid to the hired labour was recorded whereas in case of family labour, the amount was calculated on the basis of the prevailing local wage rates. When the hired labour was paid in kind either wholly or partly its money equivalent was worked out. The labour for feeding rabbits, bringing feed and fodder, watering and cleaning the shed, shearing was included.

The expenditure on transportation of feed was included in the cost of feed itself.

Labour charges were included in the variable cost as there were only a few farmers who had hired labour on their farms. Most of the farmers attended to the different operations at the farm themselves with the mutual assistance of their family members. Rationalisation of labour was done by taking one male hour (over 16 years) equivalent to one adult man hour, one female hour (over 16 years) equivalent to 0.67 hours of an adult man hour and one child hour (12–16 years) equivalent to 0.50 hours of an adult man hour (Ashok Kumar, 1988).

3.6.2.4 Computation of returns

The gross returns in rabbitry included the value of wool, sale of animals, for breeding, wool & meat and sale of manure. The net returns have been worked out by deducting total cost from the gross returns, whereas, the returns from fixed farm resources or returns over variable cost have been worked out by deducting the variable cost from gross returns. Net returns per rupee invested and benefit-cost ratio had also been worked out.

i) Gross Returns = Value of wool+value of animals sold+value of manure.

ii) Net Returns = Gross returns - Total cost.

iii) Net Returns over Variable cost = Gross returns - Variable cost.

iv) Benefit - Cost Ratio $= \frac{\text{Gross returns}}{\text{Total cost}}$

v) Net Returns per $= \frac{\text{Net returns}}{\text{Total cost}}$

rupee of investment Total cost

3.6.3 Break-even point

The break-even size of herd was calculated with the help of following formula (Rao *et al.*, 1991; Tomer *et al.*, 1992)

$$\text{Break-even point} = \frac{\text{Cost of production (Rs / farm)}}{\text{Selling price of produce (wool) Rs / rabbit}}$$

3.6.4 Input-output relationship for rabbitry

To work out the input-output relationship for wool production, linear as well as Cobb-Douglas type of production function were tried separately.

3.6.4.1 Cobb-Douglas production function

The Cobb-Douglas type of production function was tried due to its economical use of degrees of freedom and certain other advantages like, the regression co-efficients are the direct measures of elasticities of production with respect to individual input, the returns to scale are obtained directly summing the regression co-efficients and also simple for computational purpose.

The mathematical form of the function was:

$$Y = aX_1^{b1} X_2^{b2} X_3^{b3} X_4^{b4} X_5^{b5} e^u$$

Where,

Y = Wool production in rupees.

X_1 = Quantity of feed consumed in rupees.

X_2 = Quantity of fodder consumed in rupees.

X_3 = Value of medicines used in rupees.

X_4 = Labour used in man days.

X_5 = Working Capital[1] in rupees.

e^u = Error term

b_i = Elasticity co-efficients.

1) Working Capital=Electricity charges+water charges + miscellaneous expenses.

3.6.4.2 Linear production function

For the same set of explanatory variables the Linear Production Function has also been tried. The model of the following form was employed.

$$Y = a + b_i X_1 + b_2 X_2 + b_3 X_3 + b_4 X_4 + b_5 X_5 + e^u.$$

Here bi is regression coefficient and X_1 is independent variable which have already been defined under Cobb-Douglas Production Function.

In linear production function bi represent the marginal physical products of respective X_1.

To know the extent to which all the explanatory variables affect the dependent variable, the co-efficient of multiple determination (R^2) was computed. The value of R^2 also increases as the number of variables in the function increase. Thus, to overcome this lacuna adjusted R^2 ($\overline{R}^2$) was calculated as follows:

$$\overline{R}^2 = 1 - \left(1 - R^2\right)\frac{n-1}{n-k-1}$$

where,

R = Adjusted co-efficient of multiple determination.

R = Co-efficient of multiple determination.

n = Number of observations.

k = Number of parameters to be estimated excluding constant term.

The returns to scale were worked out by summing up the elasticity co-efficients of auxillary variables.

The significance of R^2 was tested by employing F=test as follows:

$$F = \frac{R^2 /(K-1)}{1-R^2 /(n-K)} \sim v_1 / v_2 \text{ d.f}$$

3.7 Problems of Rabbit Farmers

The problems and constraints confronted by rabbit entrepreneurs have been categorised into different sub-heads *viz;* production, financial, marketing and institutional problems. The per cent response was recorded on different size of rabbit farms. To test the difference in the extent of problems confronted on different size of farms, chi-square test was employed to test the rejection or acceptance of the following null hypothesis.

$H_0 : P_{ij} 1 = P_i 2 = P_i 3 = P_i 4$

P_{ij} = Problems on different categories of farms.

The value of Chi-square was computed as follows:

$$n\left[\frac{\Sigma^k}{I=1}\frac{\Sigma^k}{j=1}\frac{fij^2}{fionj}-1\right]\sim \chi^2_{(k-1)(1-1)}\ \text{df.}$$

Where,

$$Fio = \frac{\Sigma}{J=i} fij \qquad \text{(i.e. row total)}$$

$$n_j = \frac{\Sigma}{i=1} fij \qquad \text{(i.e. column total)}$$

3.8 Trends in Wool Production

To compute the growth in wool production the data for total wool production in Himachal Pradesh was obtained from the different issues of Statistical Outline of Himachal Pradesh published by Directorate of Economics and Statistics, Government of Himachal Pradesh. Due to non-availability of data of total rabbit wool production in Himachal Pradesh, the growth rates were computed for total wool production in Himachal Pradesh which includes the rabbit wool too. The data for total wool production were collected for a period of 20 years from 1978–79 to 1997–98. The linear as well as compound growth rates were computed. The production functions of the following types were employed.

Linear $Y = a + bt$

Exponential $Y = ab^t$, which in Logarithm form can be written as:

$$\text{Log } Y = \text{Log } a + t \text{ Log } b.$$

Where,

Y= Annual total wool production in Himachal Pradesh in tonnes.

t = Number of years.

a and b are regression parameters.

The growth rates from the above production functions were estimated as follows.

$$\text{Relative linear growth rate (RLGR)} = \frac{\hat{b}}{\bar{Y}} (100)$$

$$\text{Compound growth rate (CGR)} = \left(\hat{b} - 1\right) (100)$$

The standard errors for linear and compound growth rates were worked out by following algorithm:

$$\text{SE(RLGR)} = \sqrt{\frac{\Sigma Y^2 - \hat{b}\,\Sigma ty}{(N-2)\,\Sigma^{t^2}}}$$

$$\text{SE(CGR)} = \frac{(100)\left(\hat{b}\right)}{0.43429} \sqrt{\frac{\Sigma \log y^2 - \text{Log } \hat{b}\, \Sigma\, t \log y}{(N-2)\,\Sigma^{t^2}}}$$

Whereas,

$$\Sigma \log y^2 = \Sigma \log Y^2 - \frac{\left(\Sigma \log Y^2\right)}{N}$$

4

SOCIO-ECONOMIC AND STRUCTURAL PARAMETERS OF RABBIT ENTREPRENEURS

4.1 Socio-Economic and Structural Indicators

The insight into social, economic and structural parameters of rabbit entrepreneurs is important to have their background, educational level and existing status on different aspects of life. To have acquaintance with rabbit entrepreneurs on these aspects will be of great relevance in providing the guidelines for the development and growth of rabbit industry.

4.1.1 Age-wise distribution

The study of the age-wise distribution of rabbit entrepreneurs showed that majority of them were young and were in the age-group of 30–60 years followed by age group of 20–30

TABLE 4.1: Agewise distribution of rabbit entrepreneurs in Himachal Pradesh

Age in years	*Small*	*Medium*	*Large*	*All Farms*
Less than 20	7 (7.61)	–	–	7 (4.12)
20–30	37 (40.22)	12 (26.09)	7 (21.87)	56 (32.94)
30–60	46 (50.00)	29 (63.04)	23 (71.88)	98 (57.65)
60>	2 (2.17)	5 (10.87)	2 (6.25)	9 (5.29)
Total	**92 (100)**	**46 (100)**	**32 (100)**	**170 (100)**

Source: Primary data from the rabbit entrepreneurs.

Note: Figures in parentheses indicate percentage to total.

years. Rabbitry as a profession in Himachal Pradesh is not older than two decades and this was one of the major reasons that it had been taken-up by youngsters.

4.1.2 Educational level

The level of education plays an important role in decision making and managerial skill. Majority of the entrepreneurs, small, medium as well as large had studied at least up to high school level and 34.71 per cent of the entrepreneurs had done matriculation whereas 13 per cent of the entrepreneurs were degree holders (Table 4.2). The educational status of all the family members of rabbit entrepreneurs has been depicted in Table 4.3. The study of the table revealed that majority of the members had studied up to high school and constituted 26.12 per cent among all members. The next highest number of members of their families had studied up to primary level and constituted 20.48 per cent of family members.

TABLE 4.2 : Educational status of rabbit entrepreneurs in Himachal Pradesh

(per cent)

No.	*Educational* **level**	*Size of Farm*			
		Small	*Medium*	*Large*	*All Farms*
1.	Illiterate	5.43	15.22	6.25	8.24
2.	Primary	7.61	17.39	21.87	12.94
3.	Middle	13.04	17.39	12.50	14.12
4.	High School	36.96	31.61	31.25	34.71
5.	Secondary Education	20.65	10.87	3.13	14.70
6.	Degree	15.22	4.35	18.75	12.94
7.	Technical	1.09	2.17	6.25	2.35
	Total	**92 (100)**	**46 (100)**	**32 (100)**	**170 (100)**

Source: Primary data from the rabbit entrepreneurs.

TABLE 4.3 : Educational status of rabbit entrepreneurs and their family member in Himachal Pradesh

(per cent)

No.	*Educational level*	*Size of Farm*			
		Small	*Medium*	*Large*	*All Farms*
1.	Illiterate	15.05	22.69	13.86	16.92
2.	Primary	19.79	22.69	19.28	20.48
3.	Middle	14.62	21.43	17.47	17.03
4.	High School	30.54	18.07	25.30	26.12
5.	Secondary Education	9.03	7.98	8.43	8.63
6.	Degree	9.68	7.14	12.65	9.55
7.	Technical	1.29	–	2.41	1.15
8.	Others	–	–	0.60	0.12
	Total	**92 (100)**	**46 (100)**	**32 (100)**	**170 (100)**

Source: Primary data from the rabbit entrepreneurs.

4.1.3 Occupational distribution

Table 4.4 depicts the occupational pattern of rabbit entrepreneurs. Majority of the farmers (72.94%) had taken up rabbitry as their secondary profession. However, 5.29 per cent of the farmers had adopted rabbitry as a primary profession. Among main occupations agriculture was the main occupation of the farmers. 50.59 per cent of rabbit entrepreneurs had taken-up agriculture as main occupation.

4.1.4 Size of land holding

The per farm average size of net operational holding of rabbit entrepreneurs was estimated to 11.87 *kanals*. The perusal of Table 4.5 reveal that holding size on different categories of farms ranged between 11.80 to 12.97 *kanals* showing thereby very less

TABLE 4.4 : Occupational structure of rabbit entrepreneurs in HimachalPradesh

(per cent)

No.	Educational level	Size of Farm			All Farms
		Small	Medium	Large	
1. Main occupation					
	i) Rabbitry	–	8.70	15.67	5.29
	ii) Agriculture	44.57	56.52	59.38	50.59
	iii) Service	42.39	21.74	9.38	30.59
	iv) Business	13.04	13.04	15.67	13.53
	Total	**92 (100)**	**46 (100)**	**32 (100)**	**170 (100)**
2. Subsidiary occupation					
	i) Rabbitry	61.96	86.96	84.38	72.94
	ii) Agriculture	8.70	8.70	9.37	8.82
	iii) No Secondary occupation	29.34	4.34	6.25	18.24
	Total	**92 (100)**	**46 (100)**	**32 (100)**	**170 (100)**

Source: Primary data from the rabbit entrepreneurs.

variation among different classes of rabbit entrepreneurs. The area under permanent pastures was worked out to be 0.98 *kanal* per farm on all farm situations. The area under orchard was found to be 2.61 *kanals* per farm.

4.1.5 Training in Rabbitry

The institutions like Himachal Pradesh Agricultural University (Chaudhary Sarwan Kumar Himachal Pradesh Krishi Vishvavidyalaya, Palampur), the government rabbit farms and some progressive private rabbit breeders provide training to the existing

TABLE 4.5: Average size of land holding of rabbit entrepreneurs in Himachal Pradesh

(*Kanals*/farm)

No.	*Particulars*	*Size of Farm*			*All Farms*
		Small	*Medium*	*Large*	
1.	Owned land	12.10	12.06	12.97	11.97
2.	Leased-in	–	0.11	–	0.03
3.	Leased-out	0.05	0.37	–	0.13
4.	Net operational holding	12.05	11.80	12.97	11.87
5.	Fallow land	0.04	–	–	0.02
6.	Permanent pastures	0.27	2.83	0.37	0.98
7.	Orchards	1.64	1.49	9.25	2.61

Source: Primary data from the rabbit entrepreneurs.

Note: 25 *kanals* = 1 hectare.

and potential rabbit entrepreneurs on various aspects of rabbitry management. Table 4.6 shows that about 80 per cent of total rabbit entrepreneurs got a formal training. Maximum number of rabbit entrepreneurs (48.52 per cent) got a training of about a week. The rabbit entrepreneurs were of the view that a training of a week was sufficient for starting a rabbitry.

4.1.6 Investment pattern

Rabbit entrepreneurs required capital for investment on sheds, cages, breeding boxes, light fittings, water supply and various equipments. The values represented the original cost at the time of establishment of unit and further additions, if any. Details of the capital investment on the rabbit farms were computed on the basis of per 100 animals.

TABLE 4.6 : Training acquired by rabbit entrepreneurs for rabbit rearing in Himachal Pradesh

(per cent)

No.	*Duration*	*Size of Farm*			*All Farms*
		Small	*Medium*	*Large*	
1.	Nil	8.60	35.56	28.13	19.53
2.	1–7	35.48	60.00	68.75	48.52
3.	8–15	55.92	4.44	3.12	31.95
4.	16–30	–	–	–	–
5.	Above 30	–	–	–	–
	Total	**92 (100)**	**46 (100)**	**32 (100)**	**170 (100)**

Source: Primary data from the rabbit entrepreneurs.

It can be seen from the Table 4.7 that there existed a negative relationship between size of farms and investment. The investment was computed as Rs. 2,34,780, Rs. 46,437, Rs. 29,754 and Rs. 41,059 on small, medium, large and all farms respectively. The major share of capital investment was devoted to rabbit sheds and accounted for 59.62 per cent of total capital investment. The investment on cages was the next important item and constituted 26.29 per cent of investment on all farms.

TABLE 4.7 : Average capital investment per 100 rabbits on rabbit farms

(per cent)

No.	*Particulars*	*Size of Farm*			*All Farms*
		Small	*Medium*	*Large*	
1.	Land	18.79	10.95	3.81	8.66
2.	Rabbit shed	70.27	61.99	54.73	59.62
3.	Cages	7.34	22.32	35.04	26.29
4.	Breeding Boxes	0.22	0.43	0.36	0.35
5.	Feeders	0.62	1.29	2.40	1.76
6.	Waterers	0.84	1.46	3.01	2.17
7.	Light Fittings	1.23	1.15	0.52	0.83
8.	Water Supply	0.42	0.25	0.07	0.19
9.	Other equipments	0.27	0.16	0.06	0.13
	Total	**2,34,780 (100)**	**46,437 (100)**	**29,754 (100)**	**41,059 (100)**

Source: Primary data from the rabbit entrepreneurs.

4.1.7 Income from different sources

The per month income from different sources of income of rabbit entrepreneurs has been presented in Table 4.8. The table showed that the average gross income on small, medium, large and all farms situation was Rs. 6.504, 7.444, 19.217 and 9.798 on small, medium, large and all farms situation respectively. On small farms the maximum income was earned from cultivation of vegetable crops which constituted 40.49 per cent of total income, followed by service and pension (23.72%) and dairy (20.77%). On medium farms, rabbitry was the highest contributor and accounted for 34.71 per cent of total income. The next highest contribution followed by farming (15.14%). On large farms also, rabbitry was the top most contributor and its share was 65.28 per cent in total income, followed by farming (9.31%) and business (6.24%). On all farms situation the rabbitry accounted for 40.22 per cent of gross income followed by vegetable cultivation (14.35%) and service and pension (12.80%). The contribution of fruits was minimum and accounted for 3.32 per cent of total income on the all farm situation.

TABLE 4.8 : Per month gross income of rabbit entrepreneurs from different sources in Himachal Pradesh

(per cent)

No.	Particulars	Size of Farm			All Farms
		Small	Medium	Large	
1.	Farming	4.99	15.14	9.31	10.55
2.	Vegetable	40.49	8.22	3.93	14.35
3.	Fruits	–	3.73	5.52	3.32
4.	Rabbitry	4.12	34.71	65.28	40.22
5.	Dairy	20.77	15.02	6.24	12.36
6.	Business	5.90	5.59	7.04	6.40
7.	Service/pension	23.72	17.59	2.68	12.80
	Total	**6,504 (100)**	**7,444 (100)**	**19,217 (100)**	**9,798 (100)**

Source: Primary data from the rabbit entrepreneurs.

4.1.8 Consumption of Feed

Per farm per day consumption of feed on different categories of farms has been depicted in Table 4.9. The perusal of table revealed that per farm per day consumption of feed on all farms situation was 10.17 kg. However, on large farms, the consumption of feed was 37.44 kilogram per farm per day. The consumption of feed increased with the increase in size. The per rabbit per ciay feed consumption on different categories of farms has been estimated and presented in Table 4.10. The per rabbit per day feed consumption and size of farms were negatively correlated. It was 140, 130 and 120 grams respectively on small, medium and large farms respectively.

Table 4.11 shows the value of feed fed to rabbits per farm per day. The value of feed increased with the increase in size of farm and it was Rs 7.73, 60.55, 244.05 and 74.61 on small, medium, large and all farms situation respectively. Table 4.12 shows the value of total feed fed per rabbit per farm and it was computed as Rs 0.89 on all farms situation. The value of feed included the cost of transportation too.

TABLE 4.9 : Per farm feed consumption on different size of farms

(kg/day)

No.	*Particulars*	*Size of Farm*			*All Farms*
		Small	*Medium*	*Large*	
1.	Chamba	0.62	–	–	0.62
2.	Hamirpur	–	7.20	–	7.20
3.	Kangra	1.98	11.87	23.50	8.92
4.	Kinnaur	0.46	–	–	0.46
5.	Kullu	2.65	9.05	45.56	18.99
6.	Mandi	1.26	8.23	35.75	22.83
7.	Shimla	0.76	–	–	0.76
8.	Solan	1.46	8.75	–	1.72
	H.P.	**1.31**	**8.94**	**37.44**	**10.17**

Source: Primary data from the rabbit entrepreneurs.

TABLE 4.10 : Per rabbit quantity of feed consumption on different size of farms

(kg/day)

No.	Particulars	Size of Farm			All Farms
		Small	Medium	Large	
1.	Chamba	0.10	–	–	0.10
2.	Hamirpur	–	0.13	–	0.13
3.	Kangra	0.16	0.14	0.10	0.14
4.	Kinnaur	0.10	–	–	0.10
5.	Kullu	0.15	0.13	0.14	0.14
6.	Mandi	0.11	0.12	0.11	0.11
7.	Shimla	0.12	–	–	0.12
8.	Solan	0.15	0.17	–	0.15
	H.P.	**0.14**	**0.13**	**0.12**	**0.13**

Source: Primary data from the rabbit entrepreneurs.

TABLE 4.11 : Per farm value of total feed on different size of farms

(Rupees/farm/day)

No.	Particulars	Size of Farm			All Farms
		Small	Medium	Large	
1.	Chamba	4.41	–	–	4.41
2.	Hamirpur	–	49.68	–	49.68
3.	Kangra	13.66	77.82	155.10	59.41
4.	Kinnaur	3.45	–	–	3.45
5.	Kullu	4.20	60.83	299.47	125.54
6.	Mandi	2.33	58.48	231.99	150.21
7.	Shimla	5.70	–	–	5.70
8.	Solan	9.02	43.87	–	10.29
	H.P.	**7.73**	**60.55**	**244.05**	**74.61**

Source: Primary data from the rabbit entrepreneurs.

TABLE 4.12 : Per rabbit value of total feed on different size of farms

(Rupees/rabbit/day)

No.	*Particulars*	*Size of Farm*			*All Farms*
		Small	*Medium*	*Large*	
1.	Chamba	0.70	–	–	0.70
2.	Hamirpur	–	0.87	–	0.87
3.	Kangra	1.12	0.94	0.70	0.72
4.	Kinnaur	0.75	–	–	0.75
5.	Kullu	0.24	0.85	0.94	0.90
6.	Mandi	0.21	0.82	0.70	0.80
7.	Shimla	0.90	–	–	0.90
8.	Solan	0.92	0.85	–	0.91
	H.P.	**0.95**	**1.28**	**0.76**	**0.89**

Source: Primary data from the rabbit entrepreneurs.

4.1.9 Gender employment in rabbitry

The rabbitry as a profession has also been adopted by women. However, their percentage as compared to men is low. Maximum number of women had been employed in rabbitry in district solan of Himachal Pradesh and accounted for 58.58 per cent of total persons employed in rabbitry. In this district the rabbits were distributed free of cost to the trainees in a training imparted by government agencies. The women among trainees were prominent and therefore, women entrepreneurs were more than men in district Solan. No women entrepreneur was found in districts of Hamirpur and Kullu. The overall scenario of the gender employment showed that about 79 per cent of entrepreneurs were men and 21 per cent were women. The average number of men and women entrepreneurs in rabbitry profession in different districts of Himachal Pradesh has been depicted in Table 4.13.

4.1.10 Mortality in Rabbits

The mortality rate of rabbits on different size of farms has been depicted in Table 4.14. The table shows that per cent mortaility of wool rabbits was lower on large farms (8.94 %) as compared to medium farms about 24 per cent and small farms (44 %). It could be due to better management followed by large rabbit entrepreneurs.

TABLE 4.13 : Average number of men and women entrepreneurs in rabbitry profession

(Per cent)

No.	*District*	*Men*	*Women*
1.	Chamba	82.35	17.65
2.	Hamirpur	100.00	–
3.	Kangra	74.29	25.71
4.	Kinnaur	72.75	27.25
5.	Kullu	100.00	–
6.	Mandi	95.12	4.88
7.	Shimla	80.12	19.88
8.	Solan	41.42	58.58
	H.P.	**78.88**	**21.12**

Source: Primary data from the rabbit entrepreneurs.

TABLE 4.14 : Mortality of rabbits on different size of farms

(Per cent)

No.	*Districts*	*Size of Farm*			*All Farms*
		Small	*Medium*	*Large*	
1.	Chamba	33.33	–	–	33.33
2.	Hamirpur	50.00	39.13	–	40.26
3.	Kangra	32.26	25.47	–	25.81
4.	Kinnaur	14.29	–	–	14.29
5.	Kullu	–	17.00	16.25	16.47
6.	Mandi	–	24.90	5.74	10.92
7.	Shimla	–	–	–	–
8.	Solan	38.00	40.45	–	38.91
	H.P.	**44.27**	**23.95**	**8.94**	**14.09**

Source: Primary data from the rabbit entrepreneurs.

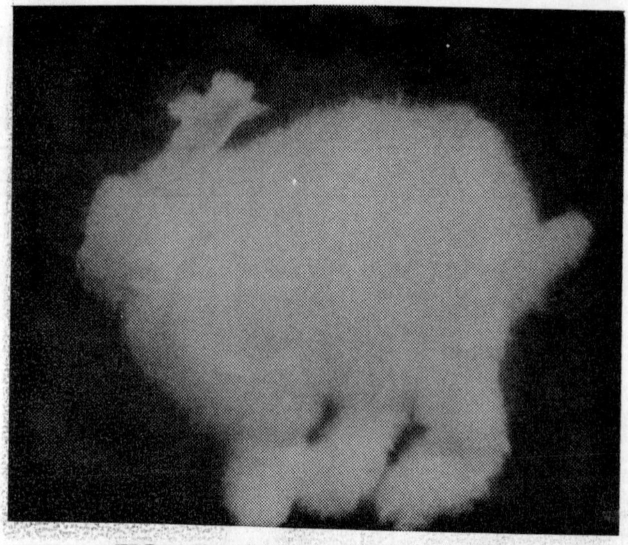

FIG.2 : Paralytic death in wool rabbits

FIG. 3 : Diarrhoeal death in wool rabbits

5

RABBIT FARMS AND WOOL PRODUCTION

5.1 Trends in Wool Production

This Chapter deals with the total wool production over the years, trends in prices and also the variation in tariffs by the Government of India over the years. In India, Angora rabbits are being reared in Himachal Pradesh and hilly areas of Uttaranchal and Uttar Pradesh. The credit of introducing and popularizing Angora rabbits in India goes to ICAR through its North Temperate Regional Institute (CSWRI) Garsa (Kullu). In 1970`s the Central Sheep and Wool Research Institute imported rabbits from USSR and UK for research and production of Angora wool, meat and fur in the country.

The CSWRI has also introduced German Angora in 1986, which is one of the best Angora breeds today which produce 800 to 1000 g wool per annum. Till now around 3000 Angora rabbits have been sold to the interested farmers for starting rabbitry units.

Himachal Pradesh is presently the largest Angora wool producing state in the country. It is estimated that out of about 30 MT per annum Angora wool production, approximately 20 MT Angora wool is produced in Himachal Pradesh (Katoch, 2001). The rabbitry units are mainly located in Mandi, Kullu and Kangra districts. The State Government has two Angora rabbit breeding farms, one at Kandwari near Palampur and other at Nagwain in Mandi district and having more than 1100 breedable animals at these two farms. The rabbitry in Himachal Pradesh is about two decades old.

5.2 Establishment of Rabbit Farms in Himachal Pradesh

Existing rabbitry units in Himachal Pradesh are less than two decades old. The existing units of rabbitry started coming-up in 1984. The maximum number of units (41) were established in 1996 followed by 40 in 1998. The agencies of the government through various programmes imparted training to willing farmers and distributed 10 rabbits and equipments free of cost to each trained farmer. This is the reason that during 1996 and afterwards large number of farms have come-up. However, majority of them were small farms. The year of establishment of rabbit farms in different districts of Himachal Pradesh has been presented in Table 5.1. The perusal of the table shows that maximum number of rabbit farms were in district Solan in 1996. The rabbit farms in Solan district are small and these farmers were supplied rabbits free of cost by the government agency through a project.

5.3 Rabbit Farms in Different Districts

The number of rabbit farms in different districts in three consecutive years have been depicted in Table 5.2. The number of rabbit farms in Himachal Pradesh in 1997-98 was 170 and maximum number was in Solan. In the second year of study 1998-99, the maximum number of rabbit farms were in Mandi district followed by Solan. In the third year of study 1999-2000 the maximum number of rabbit farms was in Mandi district (41) followed by Kullu district (22) of Himachal Pradesh.

5.4 Changing Scenario of Rabbit Farms

The fall in the price of the rabbit wool over the years has led to closing down of rabbit farms. The change in number of rabbit farms in different districts over the study period has been presented in Table 5.3. The examination of the table revealed that there had been no change in the number of rabbit farms in Mandi and Hamirpur districts of Himachal Pradesh. The next minimum closure was in Kullu district (15.38 %) of Himachal Pradesh. The maximum change in number of rabbit farms was observed in Solan district of Himachal Pradesh where the number of rabbit farms decreased from 55 to 12 and showed a change of 78.18 per cent. The next highest change was observed in Chamba district of Himachal Pradesh and accounted for 73.68 per cent. The table further shows that total number of rabbit farms decreased from 170 to 96 and showing a decline of 43.52 per cent.

TABLE 5.1 : Establishment of rabbit farms in differemt districts of Himachal Pradesh

No.	*Districts*	*1984*	*1985*	*1986*	*1987*	*1988*	*1989*	*1990*	*1991*	*1992*	*1993*	*1994*	*1995*	*1996*	*1997*	*1998*	*1999*	*Total*
1.	Chamba	–	–	–	–	–	–	–	–	–	–	–	–	–	–	–	19	19
2.	Hamirpur	–	–	–	–	–	–	–	–	–	–	–	–	–	1	3	1	5
3.	Kangra	–	–	–	1	2	2	–	1	1	–	1	1	1	–	6	–	16
4.	Kullu	3	2	1	–	1	–	1	–	1	1	1	1	5	5	4	–	26
5.	Kinnaur	–	–	–	–	–	–	–	–	–	–	–	–	–	5	–	–	5
6.	Mandi	2	–	–	1	2	–	–	2	1	1	6	4	10	4	8	–	41
7.	Shimla	–	–	–	–	–	–	–	–	–	–	–	–	3	–	–	–	3
8.	Solan	–	–	–	–	–	–	–	–	–	–	–	1	25	7	19	3	55
	H.P.	**5**	**2**	**1**	**2**	**5**	**2**	**1**	**3**	**3**	**2**	**8**	**7**	**44**	**22**	**40**	**23**	**170**

Source: Primary data from the rabbit entrepreneurs.

TABLE 5.2 : Number of rabbit farms in different districts of Himchal Pradesh

No.	Districts	1997–98				1998–99				1999–2000			
		Small	*Medium*	*Large*	*Total*	*Small*	*Medium*	*Large*	*Total*	*Small*	*Medium*	*Large*	*Total*
1.	Chamba	19	–	–	19	10	–	–	10	5	–	–	5
2.	Hamirpur	1	4	–	5	–	5	–	5	1	4	–	5
3.	Kangra	7	7	2	16	7	4	1	12	2	5	–	7
4.	Kinnaur	5	–	–	5	3	–	–	3	3	–	–	3
5.	Kullu	4	14	8	26	2	13	8	23	0	14	8	22
6.	Mandi	1	18	22	41	1	18	22	41	1	23	17	41
7.	Shimla	3	–	–	3	1	–	–	1	1	–	–	1
8.	Solan	53	2	–	55	30	2	–	32	11	1	–	12
	H.P.	93	45	32	170	54	42	31	127	24	47	25	96

Source: Primary data from the rabbit entrepreneurs.

TABLE 5.3 : Change in number of rabbit farms over the years

No.	*Districts*	*1997-98*	*1998-99*	*1999-2000*	*% Change*
1.	Chamba	19	10	5	73.68
2.	Hamirpur	5	5	5	–
3.	Kangra	16	12	7	56.25
4.	Kinnaur	5	3	3	40.00
5.	Kullu	26	23	22	15.38
6.	Mandi	41	41	41	–
7.	Shimla	3	1	1	66.67
8.	Solan	55	32	12	78.18
	H.P.	**170**	**127**	**96**	**43.52**

Source: Primary data from the rabbit entrepreneurs.

5.5 Rabbit Population in Different Districts of Himachal Pradesh

The number of rabbits in different districts of Himachal Pradesh has been given in Table 5.4.

It is interesting to note that the number of rabbit farms during the study period has decreased from 170 to 96 farms and showing a decline of 43.52 per cent. However, total number of rabbits in the state had increased from 14,300 rabbits in 1997-98 to 15,669 rabbits in 1999-2000 and showing an increase of 9.57 per cent. The reason for decreasing the number of rabbitry units yet increase in total number of rabbits could be attributed to closing down of small size of farms which were uneconomical however, the farms which are large and operating above the break-even point are running in profit and still increasing their flock size.

TABLE 5.4 : **Total number of rabbits in different districts of Himachal Pradesh**

No.	*Districts*	*Number of Rabbits*		
		1997-98	*1998-99*	*1999-2000*
1.	Chamba	103	25	20
2.	Hamirpur	255	425	230
3.	Kangra	839	599	457
4.	Kinnaur	23	10	7
5.	Kullu	3,649	4,620	4,415
6.	Mandi	8,786	9,676	10,390
7.	Shimla	23	5	4
8.	Solan	622	292	146
	H.P.	**14,300**	**15,652**	**15,669**

Source: Primary data from the rabbit entrepreneurs.

5.6 Total Rabbit Wool Production in Himachal Pradesh

The total rabbit wool production in different districts of Himachal Pradesh over the study period has been given in Table 5.5. The table shows that total rabbit wool production in Himachal Pradesh is about 7127 kilograms per year. The total wool production in agricultural year 1999-2000 has shown a slight decrease of 0.57 per cent over 1997-98. The total wool production in different size of farms in different districts of Himachal Pradesh is given in Table 5.6.

5.7 Trends in Total Wool Production

The total wool production including rabbit wool and sheep wool in Himachal Pradesh has been presented in Table 5.7. Since the separate data on rabbit wool production in Himachal Pradesh are not available, hence, the linear as well as compound growth rates for total wool production were computed.

TABLE 5.5 : Number of rabbits per farm in different districts of Himachal Pradesh

No.	Districts	1997-98				1998-99				1999-2000			
		Small	Medium	Large	Total	Small	Medium	Large	Total	Small	Medium	Large	Total
1.	Chamba	5.42	–	–	5.42	2.50	–	–	2.50	4.00	–	–	4.00
		(103)			(103)	(25)			(25)	(20)			(20)
2.	Hamirpur	25.00	57.50	–	51.00	–	85.00	–	85.00	20.00	52.50	–	46.00
		(25)	(230)		(255)		(425)		(425)	(20)	(210)		(230)
3.	Kangra	12.00	80.57	191.00	55.93	9.43	92.25	152.00	49.92	10.5	87.20	–	65.28
		(84)	(564)	(191)	(839)	(66)	(381)	(152)	(599)	(21)	(436)		(457)
4.	Kinnaur	4.60	–	–	4.60	3.33	–	–	3.33	2.33	–	–	2.33
		(23.00)			(23.00)	(10.00)			(10.00)	(7.00)			(7.00)
5.	Kullu	17.75	71.07	322.88	140.35	13.00	85.31	435.63	200.87	–	88.93	396.25	200.68
		(71.00)	(995)	(2583)	(3649)	(26.00)	(1109)	(3485)	(4620)		(1245)	(317)	(4415)
6.	Mandi	11.00	75.72	336.91	214.29	15.00	91.11	364.59	236.00	10.00	97.82	478.23	253.41
		(11.00)	(1363)	(7412)	(8786)	(15.00)	(1640)	(8021)	(9676)	(10.00)	(2250)	(813)	(10390)
7.	Shimla	7.66	–	–	7.66	5.00	–	–	5.00	4.00	–	–	4.00
		(23.00)			(23.00)	(5.00)			(5.00)	(4.00)			(4.00)
8.	Solan	9.75	52.50	–	11.31	6.17	53.50	–	9.12	8.45	53.00	–	12.17
		(517)	(105)		(622)	(185)	(107)		(292)	(93)	(53)		(146)
	H.P.	**9.22**	**72.38**	**328.58**	**84.62**	**6.15**	**87.19**	**376.06**	**123.24**	**7.29**	**89.29**	**452.00**	**163.22**
		(857)	**(3257)**	**(10186)**	**(14300)**	**(332)**	**(3662)**	**(11658)**	**(15652)**	**(175)**	**(4194)**	**(1130)**	**(15669)**

Note: Figures in parentheses indicate the total number of rabbits.
Source: Primary data from the rabbit entrepreneurs.

TABLE 5.6 : Total Rabbit wool production in different districts of HimachalPradesh

(Kilograms)

No.	Districts	Total wool production		
		1997-98	1998-99	1999-2000
1.	Chamba	32	10.70	8.0
2.	Hamirpur	158	240	157.60
3.	Kangra	472.01	368.10	277.50
4.	Kinnaur	8.70	5.10	2.20
5.	Kullu	1985	1961.40	2056.00
6.	Mandi	4172.80	4859.60	4547.50
7.	Shimla	6.80	1.80	1.60
8.	Solan	331.96	154.30	76.52
	H.P.	**7167.27**	**7601.00**	**7126.92**

Source: Primary data from the rabbit entrepreneurs.

TABLE 5.7 : Total wool (including sheep wool) production in Himachal Pradesh

(Tonnes)

Year	Wool Production
1978-79	1155.9
1979-80	1164.1
1980-81	1184.7
1981-82	1237
1982-83	1263
1983-84	1206
1984-85	1270
1985-86	1295
1986-87	1302
1987-88	1344
1988-89	1351
1989-90	1405
1990-91	1452
1991-92	1567
1992-93	1510
1993-94	1532
1994-95	1533
1995-96	1548
1996-97	1555
1997-98	1565

Source: Statistical outline of Himachal Pradesh.

FIG. 4 : An adult german angora rabbit

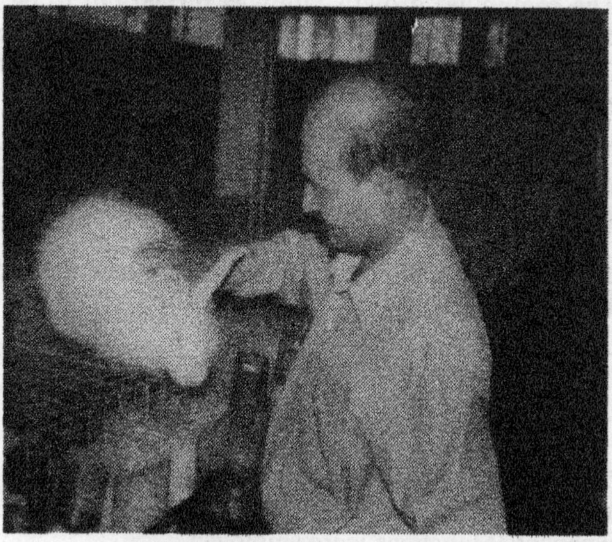

FIG. 5 : Handling of rabbit at the farm

5.7.1 Linear growth rates in total wool production

The estimated linear production function was

$Y = 1371.985 + 12.252\ t.$

Relative Linear Growth Rate = 0.893 per cent

Standard error of Linear Growth Rate = 28.049

t-value = 0.437

The test of significance shows that the linear growth rate in total wool production is non-significant at 5 per cent level of significance and showing that the total wool production in the state had not increased significantly.

5.7.2 Exponential growth rates in total wool production

The estimated exponential production was

$Y = (1364.250)\,(1.009)^t$

Compound growth rate = 0.903 per cent

Standard error = 14.886

t-value = 0.0678

The compound growth rate was turned out to be non-significant at 5 per cent level of significance, thereby revealing that wool production over the years in Himachal Pradesh had not increased significantly.

The co-efficient of variation in total wool production in Himachal Pradesh was computed as 10.87 per cent. Thereby, showing the variability of 10.87 per cent.

5.8 Trend in Rabbit Wool Procured by Himachal Pradesh State Wool Federation

The quantity of wool procured by Himachal Pradesh State Wool Federation from the rabbit entrepreneurs over the years from 1990-91 to 2001-2002 has been depicted in Table 5.8.

To compute the growth rates in the quantity of rabbit wool purchased by Himachal Pradesh State Wool Federation both linear and exponential functions were employed.

TABLE 5.8 : Rabbit wool procured by wool federation

Year	*Quantity of wool in (kg)*	*Total amount (Rs.)*	*Average Price (Rs.)*
1990-91	1585.775	7,50,299.00	473
1991-92	237.640	1,14,383.00	481
1992-93	444.300	2,33,736.00	526
1993-94	808.580	5,62,984.00	696
1994-95	1668.350	11,11,375.00	666
1995-96	3715.790	25,58,582.00	689
1996-97	3607.890	27,81,318.00	771
1997-98	4684.655	45,39,729.00	969
1998-99	10424.655	87,70,091.00	841
1999-2000	3683.505	31,04,048.00	843
2000-2001	690.995	4,79,930.00	695
2001-2002	199.995	1,37,924.00	690

Source: Himachal Pradesh State Wool Procurement and Marketing Federation, Shimla.

5.8.1 Linear growth rates in rabbit wool procured by Wool Federation

The estimated linear production function was

Y = 2646.007 + 119.811 t

Relative Linear growth rate = 4.528 per cent

Standard error of linear growth rate = 172.154

t-value = 0.437

The test of significance revealed that linear growth rate in total rabbit wool procured by Himachal Pradesh State Wool Federation is non-significant at 5 per cent level of significance. The estimated co-efficient of variation for the total quantity purchased was worked out to be 110.313 per cent thereby revealing a very high extent of variability in the quantities of wool purchased by the State Wool Federation.

TABLE 5.9 : Per farm total wool production

(Kilogram)

No.	Districts	SIZE OF FARM Ist year				2nd year				3rd year			
		Small	Medium	Large	All farms	Small	Medium	Large	All farms	Small	Medium	Large	All farms
1.	Chamba	1.68 (32.00)	–	–	1.68 (32.00)	1.07 (10.70)	–	–	1.07 (10.70)	1.60 (8.0)	–	–	1.60 (8.0)
2.	Hamirpur	15.00 (15.00)	35.75 (143.00)	–	31.60 (158.00)	–	48.00 (240.00)	–	48.00 (240.00)	13.60 (13.60)	36.00 (144.00)	–	31.52 (157.60)
3.	Kangra	6.49 (45.41)	43.94 (307.60)	119.00 (119.00)	31.46 (472.01)	5.71 (40.00)	61.02 (244.10)	84.00 (84.00)	30.67 (368.10)	6.50 (13.00)	52.90 (264.50)	–	39.64 (277.50)
4.	Kinnaur	2.90 (8.70)	–	–	2.90 (8.70)	1.70 (5.10)	–	–	1.70 (5.10)	0.73 (2.20)	–	–	0.73 (2.20)
5.	Kullu	11.50 (46.00)	37.28 (522.00)	177.12 (1417.00)	76.35 (1985.00)	4.60 (9.20)	34.09 (443.20)	188.63 (1509.00)	85.28 (1961.40)	–	32.14 (450.00)	200.75 (1606.00)	93.45 (2056.00)
6.	Mandi	4.80 (4.80)	32.89 (592.00)	162.55 (3576.00)	101.78 (4172.80)	6.40 (6.40)	42.57 (766.20)	185.77 (4087.00)	118.53 (4859.60)	4.5 (4.5)	38.35 (882.00)	215.35 (3661.00)	110.91 (4547.50)
7.	Shimla	2.26 (6.80)	–	–	2.26 (6.80)	1.80 (1.80)	–	–	1.80 (1.80)	1.60 (1.60)	–	–	1.60 (1.60)
8.	Solan	5.24 (277.96)	27.00 (54.00)	–	6.03 (331.96)	3.27 (98.30)	28.00 (56.00)	–	4.82 (154.30)	4.64 (51.02)	25.5 (25.5)	–	6.38 (76.52)
	H.P. (436.67)	**4.70 (1618.6)**	**35.97 (5112)**	**164.90 (7167.27)**	**42.41 (171.5)**	**3.18 (1749.5)**	**41.65 (5680)**	**183.23 (7601)**	**59.85 (93.92)**	**3.91 (1766)**	**37.57 (5267)**	**210.68 (7126.92)**	**74.24**

Note: Figures in parentheses indicate the total wool production in the district by different categoaries of rabbit farms.

Source: Primary data from the rabbit entrepreneurs.

5.8.2 Exponential growth in wool procured by Wool Federation

The exponential production function for the quantity of wool purchased by Himachal Pradesh State Wool Federation was

$$Y = (1433.441)\,(1.031)^t$$

Compound growth rate = 3.104 per cent

Standard error = 34.775

t-value = 0.0296

The compound growth rate was turned out to be non-significant at 5 per cent level of significance, thereby showing that the quantity of rabbit wool purchased by Himachal Pradesh State Wool Production has not increased significantly over the years.

The average price of the rabbit wool per kilogram given by Himachal Pradesh State Wool Federation in different years has been given in Table 5.8.

The co-efficient of variation for the price data was computed as 21.62 per cent to see the increase in the price the linear as well as compound growth rates were computed. Both the growth rates were turned out to be non-significant at 5 per cent level of significance, thereby revealing that the prices over the years have not increased. As increased price acts as an incentive for the production.

5.9 Customs Tariff Duty on Rabbit Wool

The per cent rate of customs tariff duty fixed by the Government of India over the years has been given in Table 5.10.

The perusal of the table shows that during the last decade the customs tariff duty had been lowered from 60 per cent to 15 per cent. However, if we look at the rate of duty in 1993-94 it was 85 per cent which was lowered to 15 per cent. The impact of liberalization is clearly visible that with the reduction in customs

TABLE 5.10 : Custom tariff duty on fine or coarse animal hair not carded or combed

No.	*Year*	*Per cent rate of duty*	*Prevailing prices in domestic market*
1.	1989-90	60	–
2.	1990-91	60	473.14
3.	1991-92	60	481.33
4.	1992-93	60	526.08
5.	1993-94	85	696.26
6.	1994-95	N.A.	666.15
7.	1995-96	50	688.56
8.	1996-97	50	770.90
9.	1997-98	50	969.06
10.	1998-99	20	841.28
11.	1999-2000	20	842.69
12.	2000-2001	15	694.55
13.	2001-2002	15	689.77

Source: Jain, R.K., *Customs Tariff of India*, Centax Publications, New Delhi.

tariff duty the access of international exporter has increased and prices in domestic market are falling. The impact of customs tariffs on prices of the domestic market in some of the year is clearly visible. In the year 1993-94, when customs tariff was increased from 60 to 85 per cent, the prices increased from Rs. 526 to Rs. 696. However, in some of the years the customs duty has not changed (duty 1997-98) but the prices have increased thereby showing that prices are also influenced by other factors than customs tariffs. In India fine wool is imported from Australia, Canada, China, France, Korea, New Zealand, USA and Switzerland.

5.10 Meaning of Fine Animal Hair in International Trade

Meaning of Fine Animal Hair in International Trade Classification– Harmonised System Code, Fine animal hair, Means the hair of Alpaca, Ilama, Vicuna, Camel, Yak, Angora, Tibetan, Kashmir or similar goats (but not common goats), rabbit (including Angora rabbit) hare, beaver, nutria or musk-rate.

5.11 Factors Affecting Wool Production

The major factors affecting wool production are:

1. *Breeds/strains:* The major factor affecting Angora wool production is the effect of breed/strain. In India Angora farming has been adopted by the farmers, commercial concerns and research/development agencies for the last two decades and the different breeds are being reared and the salient wool production and qualitative traits are given below:
2. *Heritability:* The heritability of wool production is quite high ranging from 0.6 to 0.8.
3. *Body weight:* There is a positive correlation between body weight of rabbit and quantity of wool produced.
4. *Sex:* Female rabbits generally produce more wool than the males and the difference is about 20–30 per cent.
5. *Shearing interval:* Shorter shearing interval may produce more annual wool but the fibre length remains short.
6. *Nutrition:* The balanced feed having optimum quality of energy, essential amino acids especially sulphur containing amino acids produce more wool.
7. *Age:* Wool production per kilogram of body weight increases upto 2–3 years and then starts declining at the rate of 5–10 % annually.
8. *Season and Temperature:* In moderate climatic conditions the wool yield is more than in severe summer and winter seasons.
9. *Hair density:* More number of hairs per mm^2 of body surface increases the annual wool production.
10. *Shearing methods:* Plucking/pulling of wool and machine shearing will yield more wool than ordinary scissors clipping.

6

INFRASTRUCTURE FACILITIES

6.1 Economics of wool production

Economics of wool production in a hilly state of Himachal Pradesh where the holdings are small and majority of the farmers are marginal. The supplementary enterprises such as rabbitry which is also eco-friendly can go a long way in increasing income and employment opportunities. Rabbits are economical because of early maturity, prolificacy, short gestation period of one month only. Also from climatic point of view, Himachal Pradesh is ideally suited for breeding of Angora and broiler rabbits. The rabbit industry despite its potential and congenial climatic conditions could not come up to the mark in Himachal Pradesh. In the early eighties the rabbit industry for meat started becoming popular, but in late eighties when Angora rabbits were introduced, they were found to be highly profitable as compared to meat rabbits. As a result, rabbit entrepreneurs switched over to wool rabbits and over the time meat rabbit farms were eliminated. In initial stages, when new wool rabbitry units started coming-up, the sale of wool and young rabbits for breeding purpose fetched a high price and lucrative profits for entrepreneurs. Later on, the Government of India reduced import duty on import of rabbit wool. The imported wool was available to industrialists at a cheaper rate than home produced and its price in Himachal Pradesh fell to as low as Rs. 650 per kg and resulted in recession in this industry. At this low price people were compelled not to sell their produce. Secondly, the private dealers started barter system of exchanging rabbit wool for rabbit feed and rabbit farmers share in consumer rupee was further reduced. However, with the establishment of State Wool Federation in Himachal

Pradesh this industry started reviving but later on due to low demand of wool it is at present in recession phase.

The economics of rabbit keeping is influenced by number of parameters including basic infrastructural facilities. Therefore, it is important to have knowledge of all those parameters.

6.2 Basic Infrastructural Facilities on Rabbit Farms

Basic infrastructural facilities are important for transportation, veterinary assistance and other technical guidance needed from time to time. The basic infrastructural facilities available on rabbit farms were as under :

6.2.1 Metalled Road

The majority of the rabbit farms were on the metalled road. On all farm situation about 67 per cent of rabbit farms were having distance less than one kilometre. Only four (2.3 per cent) rabbit farms, that too in small category, were having distance of more than 5 kilometres from metalled road.

6.2.2 Nearest Town

About 44 per cent of the rabbit farms were away from the town by a distance of more than 5 kilometre. Twenty one per cent of the rabbit farms were within a radius of one kilometre.

6.2.3 Railway Station

This facility was not available to majority of rabbit farms. Only four rabbit farms (2.37%) were within the radius of one kilometre.

6.2.4 Veterinary Centre

Veterinary centre for majority of the rabbit farms (34.32%) was away from the radius of 5 kilometres. Twenty per cent of rabbit farms on all farms situation were within a radius of one kilometre.

6.2.5 Medical Store

The location of medical store was important for the purchase of medicines when needed in emergency. The medical stores were located at a distance of less than one kilometre for 13.02 per cent of farmers. However, about 45 per cent of farms were located at a distance of more than 5 kilometres.

6.2.6 Bus Stand

Majority of the farms (53 %) were located at a distance of less than one kilometre from the bus stand. Only 5.92 per cent of farms were at a distance of more than 5 kilometre.

6.2.7 Bank

The branch of the bank for 45 per cent of rabbit farms was located at a distance of more than 5 kilometre. The next highest per cent of farms (19 %) were at a distance of 1–2 kilometre from the bank.

6.2.8 Co-operative Store

The co-operative store was located at a distance of less than one kilometre for 49 per cent of the farms. The next highest percentage of farms (18 %) were located at a distance of 1–2 kilometre from the co-operative store.

6.2.9 Post Office

Most of the rabbit farms were located at a distance of 1–2 kilometre from the post office. Only 12 per cent of rabbit farms were at a distance of more than 5 kilometre.

6.2.10 Source of Feed

The source of feed availability for about 53 per cent of the farms was at a distance of more than 5 kilometre. As against 19.53 per cent who had a source of feed at a distance of less than one kilometre.

6.2.11 Office of Block Development Officer

The block headquarter for majority of the farmers (78.11%) was at a distance of more than 5 kilometre.

6.2.12 Facility of Breeding Centre

In rabbit production the cross breeding is a pre-requisite to attain a vigour, good health and returns from animals. The cross breeding facility for majority of the farms was available at a distance of less than one kilometre (71%).

6.2.13 Market for Sale of Wool

For majority of the farms (65.68%) the market for sale of wool was available at distance of more than 5 kilometre.

6.3 Cost of Rearing of Wool Rabbits

The cost per annum of rearing a unit of 100 rabbits has been computed. The total cost component has been bifurcated into fixed and variable costs. Fixed cost includes interest on fixed capital and depreciation on buildings, animals, cages and equipments. Variable cost includes expenses on feed, fodder, medicines, labour and miscellaneous expenses. Miscellaneous expenses include expenses on purchase of breeding rabbits, electricity and water. The total cost of rearing a unit of 100 rabbits came out to be Rs. 1,24,968, 69,232, 51,336 and Rs. 71,513 on small, medium, large and all farms situation.

On small farms the total fixed cost constituted 36.48 per cent of total cost. The major component of fixed cost was interest on fixed capital and accounted for about 23 per cent of total cost. The depreciation on equipments had minimum share in fixed cost and accounted for 0.68 per cent of total cost. Among variable cost the expenses on feed were the main component and accounted for about 27 per cent of total cost. The next highest expenses were on labour which accounted for about 25 per cent of total cost.

On medium farms fixed and variable costs accounted for about 20 and 80 per cent of total cost respectively. Among the items of fixed cost, interest on fixed capital and depreciation on animals were the major constituents which accounted for about 8 per cent each. Among variable cost, the expenses on feed was the major item and constituted about 52 per cent of total cost. The next highest expenses were on labour which constituted about 15 per cent of total cost. The expenses on fodder were to the tune of 10.18 per cent.

There was marginal variations in the fixed and variable costs on large farms compared to medium farms. The depreciation on animals was the major constituent which accounted for about 10 per cent of total cost. The interest on fixed capital was the next highest item and its share was 6.93 per cent towards total cost.

On all farms situation the fixed cost and variable costs had similar pattern. In a fixed cost the depreciation on animals and interest on fixed capital were the major items which constituted about 8 and 7 per cent of the total cost. Among variable expenses the expenses on feed and labour were the major items respectively, and accounted for about 46 per cent and 22 per cent of the total cost.

It is evident from Table that in fixed cost the depreciation on animals and interest on fixed capital were the major items. However, in a variable cost the major items of expenses were feed and labour charges. The high prices of the feed led to high cost of production. In Mandi district one of the rabbit entrepreneurs had started production of feed from locally available feed resources and that feed was costing Rs. 650 per quintal as compared to Rs. 850 per quintal of feed manufactured by multinational companies. If more such feed manufacturing plants were established in different districts. This was likely to reduce the cost of production significantly.

TABLE 6.1 : Basic infrastructural facilities on rabbit farms

No.	*Particulars*	Size of Farm			
		Small	*Medium*	*Large*	*All Farm*
1	2	3	4	5	6
1.	**Metalled Road**				
	i) 0-1 km	56.98	68.89	96.77	67.46
	ii) 1-2 km	20.43	13.33	3.23	15.38
	iii) 2-3 km	5.38	2.22	–	3.55
	iv) 3-4 km	5.38	15.56	–	7.10
	v) 4-5 km	7.53	–	–	4.14
	vi) Above 5 km	4.30	–	–	2.37
2.	**Nearest Town**				
	i) 0-1 km	24.73	17.78	12.90	20.71
	ii) 1-2 km	32.26	6.67	3.23	20.11
	iii) 2-3 km	6.45	2.22	–	4.14
	iv) 3-4 km	7.53	6.67	–	5.91
	v) 4-5 km	5.38	–	3.23	3.55
	vi) Above 5 km	23.65	66.66	80.64	44.38
3.	**Railway Station**				
	i) 0-1 km	3.23	2.22	–	2.37
	ii) 1-2 km	10.75	4.44	–	7.10
	iii) 2-3 km	4.30	2.22	–	2.96
	iv) 3-4 km	1.08	–	–	0.59
	v) 4-5 km	5.38	–	–	2.96
	vi) Above 5 km	75.26	91.12	100	84.02
4.	**Veterinary Centre**				
	i) 0-1 km	27.96	11.11	6.45	19.53
	ii) 1-2 km	21.50	11.11	12.90	17.16
	iii) 2-3 km	7.53	24.44	16.13	13.61
	iv) 3-4 km	10.75	17.78	6.45	10.65
	v) 4-5 km	5.38	2.22	58.06	4.73
	vi) Above 5 km	26.88	33.34	58.06	34.32
5.	**Medical Store**				
	i) 0-1 km	19.35	2.22	9.67	13.01
	ii) 1-2 km	25.81	11.11	3.23	17.75
	iii) 2-3 km	6.45	8.89	–	5.92
	iv) 3-4 km	9.68	11.11	3.23	8.88
	v) 4-5 km	12.90	6.67	3.23	9.47
	vi) Above 5 km	25.81	60.00	80.64	44.97
6.	**Bus Stand**				
	i) 0-1 km	53.76	60.00	38.71	52.65
	ii) 1-2 km	24.73	17.78	12.90	20.71
	iii) 2-3 km	5.38	–	16.13	5.92
	iv) 3-4 km	3.23	22.22	29.03	13.02
	v) 4-5 km	2.15	–	3.23	1.78
	vi) Above 5 km	10.75	–	–	5.92

contd.

1	2	3	4	5	6
7.	**Bank**				
	i) 0-1 km	20.43	8.89	3.23	14.20
	ii) 1-2 km	26.88	11.11	6.44	18.93
	iii) 2-3 km	4.30	8.89	–	4.73
	iv) 3-4 km	8.60	13.33	3.23	8.88
	v) 4-5 km	11.83	4.45	3.23	8.29
	vi) Above 5 km	27.96	53.33	83.87	44.97
8.	**Co-operative Store**				
	i) 0-1 km	50.53	31.11	67.74	48.52
	ii) 1-2 km	18.27	26.67	3.23	17.75
	iii) 2-3 km	4.30	–	–	2.37
	iv) 3-4 km	7.52	2.22	–	4.73
	v) 4-5 km	3.25	2.22	–	2.37
	vi) Above 5 km	16.13	37.78	29.03	24.26
9.	**Post Office**				
	i) 0-1 km	33.33	35.56	9.67	29.58
	ii) 1-2 km	32.26	26.67	32.26	30.76
	iii) 2-3 km	9.68	11.11	3.23	8.88
	iv) 3-4 km	7.53	11.11	9.68	8.88
	v) 4-5 km	6.45	6.66	22.58	9.47
	vi) Above 5 km	10.75	8.89	22.68	12.43
10.	**Source of Feed Availability**				
	i) 0-1 km	4.30	17.78	67.74	19.53
	ii) 1-2 km	10.75	6.66	–	7.69
	iii) 2-3 km	7.53	2.22	–	4.73
	iv) 3-4 km	3.22	11.11	–	4.73
	v) 4-5 km	5.38	15.56	19.36	10.66
	vi) Above 5 km	68.82	46.67	12.90	52.66
11.	**BDO Office**				
	i) 0-1 km	–	–	9.68	4.73
	ii) 1-2 km	5.38	2.22	–	7.10
	iii) 2-3 km	11.83	–	–	3.35
	iv) 3-4 km	6.45	2.22	–	0.59
	v) 4-5 km	7.53	6.67	–	5.92
	vi) Above 5 km	68.81	88.89	64.52	78.11
12.	**Nearest Breeding Centre Facility**				
	i) 0-1 km	75.27	51.11	87.10	71.01
	ii) 1-2 km	5.38	–	–	2.96
	iii) 2-3 km	2.15	2.22	–	1.77
	iv) 3-4 km	1.08	–	–	0.59
	v) 4-5 km	–	2.22	–	0.59
	vi) Above 5 km	16.12	44.45	12.90	23.08
13.	**Market for Sale of Wool**				
	i) 0-1 km	4.30	31.11	67.74	23.08
	ii) 1-2 km	–	2.22	3.23	1.18
	iii) 2-3 km	4.30	11.11	3.23	5.92
	iv) 3-4 km	–	2.22	3.23	1.18
	v) 4-5 km	4.30	–	3.23	2.96
	vi) Above 5 km	87.10	53.34	19.34	65.68

6.4 Returns and Benefit Cost Ratio

Table 6.2 shows the returns and benefit-cost analysis on different size of rabbit farms. A close perusal of the table reveals that wool was the major source of income accounting for about 76 per cent of the gross returns, followed by sale of animals (19.70%) and value of manure (4.21%) on all farms situation. The gross returns increased with increase in farm size. The net returns were found to be negative on small and medium farm. On these two farm situations the net returns over variable cost were also found to be negative.

TABLE 6.2 : Cost of rearing rabbits on different categories of farms

(Rupees/100 rabbits)

Cost Items	Size of Farm			All Farm
	Small	Medium	Large	
A. Fixed Cost				
1. Interest on fixed capital	28174 (22.54)	5572 (8.05)	3570 (6.93)	4927 (6.89)
2. Depreciation charges				
a) Buildings	8249 (6.60)	1439 (2.08)	814 (1.58)	1224 (1.71)
b) Animals	6601 (5.28)	5340 (7.71)	5250 (10.19)	5730 (8.01)
c) Cages	1724 (1.38)	1037 (1.50)	1043 (2.02)	1079 (1.51)
d) Equipments	845 (0.68)	220 (0.32)	191 (0.37)	223 (0.31)
Sub-total:	45593 (36.48)	13608 (19.66)	10868 (21.09)	13183 (18.43)
B. Variable Cost				
1. Feed	33311 (26.66)	35846 (51.78)	31598 (61.31)	32761 (45.81)
2. Fodder	6151 (4.92)	7048 (10.18)	3689 (7.16)	5545 (7.75)
3. Medicine	4389 (3.51)	1617 (2.33)	1384 (2.96)	2359 (3.30)
4. Labour	31219 (24.98)	10114 (14.61)	3476 (6.74)	15817 (22.12)
5. Miscellaneous charges*	4305 (3.45)	999 (1.44)	521 (1.01)	1848 (2.59)
6. Sub-total:	79375 (63.52)	55624 (80.34)	40668 (78.91)	58330 (81.57)
Total cost (A+B)	**1,24,968** (100)	**69,232** (100)	**51,536** (100)	**71,513** (100)

*Includes purchase of breeding rabbits for cross-breeding purpose, electricity, water, etc.

Source: Primary data from the rabbit entrepreneurs.

The benefit-cost ratio was observed to be 0.40, 0.73, 1.00 and 0.72 on small, medium, large and all farms situations respectively.

TABLE 6.3 : Returns and benefit cost analysis on different categories of rabbit farms

(Rupees)

No.	Particulars	Size of Farm			All Farms
		Small	Medium	Large	
1.	Total Cost	1,24,968	69,232	51,536	71,513
	a. Fixed cost	45,593	13,608	10,868	13,183
	b. Variable cost	79,375	55,624	40,668	58,330
2.	Gross Returns (Rs)	50,384 (100)	50,480 (100)	51,737 (100)	51,332 (100)
	a. Wool	35,157 (69.78)	38,971 (77.20)	40,811 (78.88)	39,060 (76.09)
	b. Sale of Animals	13,032 (25.86)	9,355 (18.53)	8,791 (16.99)	10,114 (19.70)
	c. Manure	2,195 (4.36)	2,154 (4.27)	2,135 (4.13)	2,158 (4.21)
3.	Net Returns	–74,584	–18,752	201	–20,181
4.	Returns over variable cost	–28,991	–5,144	11,069	–6,998
5.	Net returns per rupee of investment	–0.60	0.27	0.004	–0.28
6.	Benefit cost ratio	0.40	0.73	1.00	0.72

Source: Primary data from the rabbit entrepreneurs.

6.5 Cost Per Kilogram of Wool Production

The per kilogram cost of wool production decreased with the increase in farm size. It was highest on small farms (Rs. 2648), followed by medium farm (Rs. 1323) and Rs. 941 on large farms. On all farms the total cost of wool production was computed as Rs. 1364 per kilogram of wool production (Table 6.4). The net returns per kilogram of wool production were negative on small and medium farms. However, they were marginally positive on large farms. At the existing level of returns the rabbit farms cannot remain in production in the long run. Even the net returns over variable cost were negative on small and medium farms. However, the large farms are making a profit of Rs. 201 per kilogram of wool over variable cost. The net returns over total cost of a kilogram of wool production were just Rs. 3 per kilogram of wool.

TABLE 6.4 : Cost of production and net returns per kilogram of wool production on rabbit farms

(Rupees/kg wool)

No.	Farm Size	Cost of Production			Gross* Returns	Net Returns	
		Fixed cost	Variable cost	Total cost		Over Variable cost	Over total cost
1.	Small	966	1682	2648	1068	–614	–1580
2.	Medium	260	1093	1323	965	–98	–358
3.	Large	198	743	941	944	201	+003
4.	All Farms	251	1113	1364	979	–134	–385

*Gross returns include sale of rabbits and manure too.
Source: Primary data from the rabbit entrepreneurs.

6.6 Break-even Analysis

The rabbitry unit may continue in production in the short run if the revenue obtained through the sale of wool, breeding and woollers animals and manure can even cover the variable cost, *i.e.*, the price of the product is equal to or higher than the average variable cost. In such a situation, the expenditure on fixed investments–buildings, machinery and salaries of the staff : are left uncovered. However, in the long it is essential that the sale of the products should cover the total cost including the expenditure on fixed investments and should leave a margin of profit. For this purpose, the break-even analysis of rabbitry units for different categories of rabbit units was done.

The per farm total cost incurred on rabbitry units was segregated into fixed and variable costs to find out the break-even output. The fixed cost included interest on fixed capital investment, depreciation on buildings and equipments. All other operational expenditures were included in variable cost.

The break-even size of the herd was calculated with the help of following formula (Rao *et al.*, 1991, Tomer et al., 1999) :

$$\text{Break} - \text{even point} = \frac{\text{Cost of production (Rs / farm)}}{\text{Selling price of wool (Rs / rabbit)}}$$

The cost of production included the fixed as well as variable cost and selling price of wool (Rs/rabbit) was worked out by multiplying the quantity of wool produced by a rabbit in a year multiplied by a price per kilogram of wool.

The break even size for small farms was worked out to be 29 against the existing size of 8 rabbits. For medium entrepreneurs the break-even size of herd was 148 against existing size 83 only. The break-even herd size for large farms was 332 against existing of 261 (Table 6.5). However, on all farms situations the break-even herd size was worked out to be 166 against the existing size of 90 rabbits. Therefore, for economic viability of rabbit farms, the entrepreneurs should increase their size of farms to reap the benefit of economies of scale.

TABLE 6.5 : Break-Even point for different categories of rabbit farms

No.	*Particulars*	*Size of Farm*			*All Farm*
		Small	*Medium*	*Large*	
1.	Cost of Production (Rs./farm)				
	a) Fixed cost	3647	11295	28365	11864
	b) Variable cost	6350	46168	106143	52497
	c) Total cost (a+b)	9997	57463	134508	64361
2.	Selling price of wool (Rs./rabbit)	349	387	405	388
3.	Break-even Size (1÷2)	29	148	332	166
4.	Existing number of rabbits per farm	8	83	261	90

Source: Primary data from the entrepreneurs.

FIG. 6 : A professive woman rabbit entrepreneur

FIG. 7 : Using local material for low cost rabbit shed

TABLE 6.6 : Extent of deviation between existing and break-even size of rabbit farms

No.	*Category*	*Existing Size of Farm*	*Break-even Size*	*Extent of deviation from optimum size (%)*
1.	Small	8	29	72.41
2.	Medium	83	148	43.92
3.	Large	261	332	21.38
4.	All farms	90	166	45.78

Source: Primary data from the rabbit entrepreneurs.

6.7 Extent of Deviation from Break-even Level

Table 6.6 shows the extent of deviation between existing and break-even size of herd on different size of farms. The close perusal of the table shows that extent of deviation and farm size has inverse relationship. The extent of deviation decreased with the increase in farm size. The maximum extent of deviation was observed on small farms (72.41%) followed by medium farms (43.92 %) and large farms (21.38%). The extent of deviation in the size of herd between existing and break-even size was worked out to be 45.78 per cent on all farms situation.

7

MARKETING CHANNELS AND MARKETING COSTS

In the present era of liberalization, privatization and globalisation the quality of the agricultural products plays vital role in marketing. Producers who are keen for quality and market their produce at appropriate time and place flourish their business. It is often seen that low prices due to glut in the market have driven farmers to despair. Marketing of agricultural products these days has become more of an art than science. To be a successful marketing manager requires knowledge and skill. Most farmers lack these skills because of an inadequate information system and poor infrastructural facilities.

Agricultural marketing calls for dynamism and a sound information system. An efficient marketing strategy is thus, a key to prosperity for the farmers. Therefore, sound marketing system can play a major role in boosting production, productivity and income. Himachal Pradesh is confronted with a blend of marketing problems.

In an attempt to solve the problems of the rabbit entrepreneurs, the Government of Himachal Pradesh established Himachal Pradesh State Co-operative Wool Procurement and Marketing Federation (WPMF) in 1988-89 which was to look after the interest of sheep and rabbit breeders in marketing of wool. Besides it, various Khadi Institutions, Non-Government Organisations and private entrepreneurs engaged in manufacturing of woollen products were also procuring Angora rabbit wool. Study of trends of Angora wool marketing revealed that prices of Angora wool fluctuated a lot. The Angora wool price had gone as high as Rs. 1400 per kg in mid 80`s, but after that it crashed down to Rs. 450 per kg. As a consequence 90 per cent of Angora units were wiped out in the state during 1989. Since January 1998 the declining graph of prices have again become a matter of grave concern to the farmers. The price of Rs. 1,000 was brought down to Rs. 925 by WPMF and now to Rs. 750 per kg of "A" grade Angora wool.

The Wool Development Board, Government of India had taken up a project for development of Angora rabbits in the country keeping in view the importance of the fibre and its potential in the employment generation. The programme having an integrated approach, had been launched in Himachal Pradesh since 1993-94 with the help of Himachal Pradesh State Wool Procurement and Marketing Federation Limited, Shimla. The main components of the project was to supply foundation stock, rabbit cages, health care, feed, marketing assistance and training to rabbit breeders. The Board intended to implement this project in the potential areas of Himachal Pradesh, Uttar Pradesh, Darjeeling (West Bengal), Nilgiri(Tamil Nadu) and hilly areas of North-East States.

The Wool Development Board had sanctioned two Industrial Service Centres to the Government of Uttar Pradesh which will be set up at Pashulok (Rishikesh) and at Pithoragrh with the technical assistance from Wool Research Association. These Industrial Service Centres will be used in preparing blends of rabbit hair, Mohair and Merino wool and fur spinning of Angora Rabbit hair, Mohair etc. on mini spinning systems. These Industrial Service Centres will also provide facilities for weaving, knitting and testing of different properties of rabbit wool and help in improving the quality of the end-products. The performance of the centers will be evaluated by the technical experts and if the technology adopted is found successful and economically viable, then such efforts will be replicated in the other areas of the country where such facilities are required.

Rabbit wool had a great marketing potential as there was no animal fibre which had the same lightness, softness and purity of fleece as Angora. The typical, weight of Angora wool would be 1.1 g per cm^3, whereas the next lightest of wool (Finest Merino) would weigh approximately 1.3 g per cm^3.

In textile terminology, the fineness could be termed in tex number which was 7 tex in Angora wool meaning thereby that it was possible to spin 1000 metres of yarn from 7 gram of Angora wool. But a tex number of 10 was more usual in ordinary Angora wool. The tex number (core spinning) for a fine sheep's wool would be of the order 20.

The softness of the Angora wool was produced by the extreme smoothness of the cuticle. This softness was such that confers a very different touch to other wool-fibres when it was blended in them even to such a small proportion of 10–15 per cent (Table 7.1). Fibre length, fibre diameter and proportion of guard hair were the main characteristics in determining the quality of wool which comprises of wooly fibres and guard hair. Guard hair were different in length and thickness which was more towards head than at tail.

TABLE 7.1 : The composition of angora fleece

Type	*Av. Length (cm)*	*Av. Diameter (microns)*		*Percentage in fleece*
		Head	*Tail*	
Guard hair (1)	12–13	80–90	50–60	0–2
Guard hair (2)	10–12	70–80	40–50	2–4
Wooly hair	8–9	60–80	20–30	15–20
Wooly fibres	5–7	15–20	10–15	70–75

All the Angora rabbit hair are modulated which are ladder shaped. This modulation can be seen under projection microscope as black streaks may be in uniformity or in different lengths. Crimping in number of crimps per centimeter. Greater the number of crimps per cm better the wool, other characteristics of course being equal. The best strains of German Angoras have probably the best ratio of 7 crimps/cm, followed by French Angoras (6) and British Angoras (5).

7.1 Angora Wool and Industrial Utilization

In fabric industry "Angora" means those fibres which are obtained from Angora rabbits. The International Standard Organisation has given `WA' abbreviation for Angora wool where `W' stands for fine animal fibre and `A' for Angora rabbit.

Angora wool is being used as a speciality animal fibre and utilized in the woollen industry mostly in fashion fabric and trade. The appropriate length of Angora wool makes the fibre in great demand in apparel industry. Due to this quality, the yam becomes firm and cohesive. Angora wool is very light, soft and fluffy and handling is slippery but due to longer fibre length it can be spun easily as pure or blended yarn. The yarn made of shorter fibres is of low tensile strength and considered to be of low grade and Angora hair being shedding off. This low grade fabric does not fetch good market price.

7.2 Angora Wool Utilization in Cottage Industry

Apart from utilizing Angora fibre in textile industrial units, it can effectively be used in cottage industry by the small farmers themselves. Angora wool can be blended, combed, carded and spun by hand/*charkha* viz., spinning by the house ladies and other members of the family. This hand spun yarn was most sought after by the local weavers for weaving of designer shawls, gents *chaddars, mufflers,* tweeds and blankets etc. Further more small farmers can also dye (Vegetable/chemical) the spun yarn and use it as knit yarn for children, ladies and gents knitwears which can fetch adequate market price.

Of the recent years there has been the development of what might be called "therapeutic garments and aids" manufactured to act as a palliative for arthritic conditions and rheumatic pains. The reasons that Angora wool should act in this way appears to be due partly to its heat retaining properties and partly to its ability to let the skin breathe easily and partly due to its peculiar electrical properties. Many sufferers from such conditions have found the relief by the use of these Angora undergarments or knit wears.

The maximum use of Angora fibre in the textile or cottage industry was being done as a blended fibre which can be mixed with other vegetative fibres, animal fibres and synthetic fibres in proportions ranging from 10 to 80 per cent. The proportion of Angora wool blend depends upon the end use of the blended yarn whether to be used as knitting yarn or for the manufacture of fine fabrics.

There appears to be a cycle in the demand of Angora wool which varies after a cycle of 5–6 years or so. At its peak very high prices (Rs. 1000 per kg in 1997) were fetched but in troughs the prices fetched were quite uneconomical. The answer to this variation in wool prices was to make maximum use of Angora fibre in cottage industry sector which could bring better economic returns and also bring the stability and security of prices during periods of slumps.

TABLE 7.2 : Market prices of angora wool

No.	*Year*	*Price (Rs.)*
1.	1980	300
2.	1981	600
3.	1982	650
4.	1983	450
5.	1984	400
6.	1985	500
7.	1986	700
8.	1987	775
9.	1988	720
10.	1989	625
11.	1990	650
12.	1991	600
13.	1992	650
14.	1993	700
15.	1994	650
16.	1995	750
17.	1996	900
18.	1997	1000
19.	1998	750
20.	1999	750
21.	2000	725
22.	2001	750

Source : Kamal Kishore and Krishma Shamshi, 2001 and primary data from rabbit entrepreneurs.

Variation in market prices of angora wool

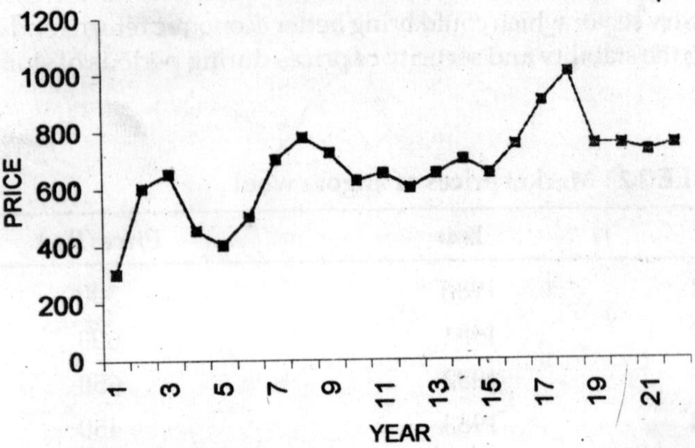

It is evident from the data and graph that the prices have shown big fluctuations over the years.

The graph shows that there has been a phenomenal rise in prices during the years from 1994 to 1997. However, the peak price of Rs. 1000 could not be attained later on. This fluctuation in wool prices resulted in increasing or decreasing the flock strength. At times when there was a great demand of wool at higher prices. The farmers could quickly build up their stocks, and if the demand decreased, the herd size could be reduced.

7.3 Marketing Functions for Rabbit Wool

Marketing of rabbit wool required careful handling, storage, packing and transportation as good quality wool fetched better prices to producers. Thus, the rabbit wool must undergo important marketing functions right from shearing till it is purchased by various agencies. These functions *inter alia* include assembling and concentration at the farm, grading, packaging, transportation, storage and marketing. The grading of rabbit wool is done on the basis of length of the fibre and cleanliness. If wool was not kept properly it gave shabby look the traders treated it as a low grade wool and fetched low-prices. Among all marketing functions the transportation involved maximum expenses.

7.4 Marketing Channels for Rabbit Wool

Marketing channels are the routes or path through which a commodity or product finds its way from producers to the ultimate consumers. Marketing channels played a vital role in disposal of produce and also the producers' share in consumers' rupee. The size and length of the channel depended upon the nature of the product and the distance between producer and consumer. There were number of intermediaries viz., local traders, commission agents, wholesalers, co-operative societies, government agencies, processing units and retailers between the producer and ultimate consumers. All these agencies had the profit earning motive though they rendered very valuable service. These were the agencies which helped in creating form, place and time utility in a product. Hence, the type of channel selected greatly affects the absolute as well as proportionate share of the producers in the consumers' rupee. The important marketing channels in the study area were:

1. Producer → Himachal Pradesh State Co-operative Wool Procurement and Marketing Federation → Hosiery → Wool Products → Consumers.
2. Producer → Hosiery → Wool Products → Consumer.
3. Producer → Hosiery → Processed Wool Products → Wholesalers Retailers → Consumers.
4. Producer → Large Producer → Hosiery → Wool Products → Consumers.
5. Producer → Traders → Hosiery → Wool Products → Consumers.
6. Producer → Trader → Rabbit yarn factory → Wool Products → Consumers.
7. Producer → Processing of rabbit wool → Wool Products → Consumers.
8. Producer → Processing of rabbit wool → Products → Commission agents → Consumers.

The adoption of the marketing channels by the rabbit entrepreneurs in different districts of Himachal Pradesh has been presented from Table 7.3 to Table 7.6.

Table 7.3 presents the main channels of marketing of rabbit wool on small farms. The perusal of the table showed that majority of the rabbit entrepreneurs marketed the wool through Himachal Pradesh State Wool Federation. However, the other conspicuous channels were through traders and large producers which also acted as traders in collection of rabbit wool and helped in further marketing.

Table 7.4 showed that on medium farms the main marketing of rabbit wool was through wool federation. However, a few farmers are also selling their rabbit wool through traders, large producers and converting them into products like shawls through self processing.

On large farms 40 per cent of rabbit entrepreneurs were selling their wool through wool federation and traders. In Kangra district wool federation and self-processing of rabbit wool was important channel. In Kullu district the majority of wool was being marketed through traders. In Mandi district the wool entrepreneurs were selling through almost all the marketing channels.

The study of marketing channels on all farms revealed that majority of rabbit entrepreneurs were marketing wool through Himachal Pradesh State Wool Federation.

7.5 Marketing Costs

The marketing costs incurred in marketing of rabbit wool included shearing charges, cost of packing material, grading charges, loading and unloading charges, transportation charges and spoilage and losses. The marketing costs incurred per kilogram of rabbit wool have been presented on different size of farms in different districts from Table 7.7 to Table 7.10.

TABLE 7.3 : Channels of marketing of rabbit wool on small farms in different districts of Himachal Pradesh

(Percentage)

No.	Channel Number	Channel	Districts							
			Chamba	*Hamirpur*	*Kangra*	*Kinnaur*	*Kullu*	*Mandi*	*Shimla*	*Solan*
1.	I	Producer-Wool Federation	52.56	57.14	–	–	–	–	66.67	40.75
2.	II	Producer-Hosiery-Consumer	5.26	–	–	–	–	–	–	18.52
3.	III	Producer-Hosiery-Wholesalers	–	–	–	–	–	–	–	–
4.	IV	Producer-Large Producers	10.52	–	–	40.00	–	–	33.33	24.07
5.	V	Producer-Traders Hosiery	10.52	-	42.86	60.00	25.00	100.00	–	12.96
6.	VI	Producer-Trader-Rabbit Yarn Factory	–	–	–	50.00	–	–	–	–
7.	VII	Producer-Self Processing-Consumers	21.04	–	–	–	25.00	–	–	3.70
8.	VIII	Producer-Processing-Commission Agent-Consumers	–	–	–	–	–	–	–	–

Source: Primary data from the rabbit entrepreneurs.

TABLE 7.4 : Channels of marketing of Rabbit wool on medium farms in different districts of Himachal Pradesh

(Percentage)

No.	Channel Number	Channel	Districts							
			Chamba	Hamirpur	Kangra	Kinnaur	Kullu	Mandi	Shimla	Solan
1.	I	Producer-Wool Federation	–	–	57.13	–	28.57	27.78	–	–
2.	II	Producer-Hosiery-Consumer	–	–	–	–	14.29	16.67	–	–
3.	III	Producer-Hosiery-Wholesalers	–	–	–	–	–	–	–	–
4.	IV	Producer-Large Producers	14.29	–	–	–	14.29	11.11	–	–
5.	V	Producer-Traders Hosiery	14.29	–	–	–	14.29	11.12	–	100.00
6.	VI	Producer-Trader-Rabbit Yarn Factory	–	–	–	–	28.56	27.78	–	–
7.	VII	Producer-Self Processing-Consumers	14.29	–	–	–	–	5.15	–	–
8.	VIII	Producer-Processing-Commission Agent-Consumer	–	–	–	–	–	–	–	–

Source: Primary data from the rabbit entrepreneurs.

TABLE 7.5 : Channels of marketing of Rabbit wool on Large farms in different districts of Himachal Pradesh

(Percentage)

No.	Channel Number	Channel	Districts							
			Chamba	*Hamirpur*	*Kangra*	*Kinnaur*	*Kullu*	*Mandi*	*Shimla*	*Solan*
1.	I	Producer-Wool Federation	–	40.00	50.00	–	12.50	18.18	–	–
2.	II	Producer-Hosiery-Consumer	–	–	–	–	–	22.73	–	–
3.	III	Producer-Hosiery-Wholesalers	–	–	–	–	–	–	–	–
4.	IV	Producer-Large Producers	–	20.00	–	–	–	27.26	–	–
5.	V	Producer-Traders Hosiery	–	40.00	–	–	50.00	13.64	–	–
6.	VI	Producer-Trader-Rabbit Yarn Factory	–	–	–	–	37.50	13.64	–	–
7.	VII	Producer-Self Processing-Consumers	–	–	50.00	–	–	4.55	–	–
8.	VIII	Producer-Processing-Commission Agent-Consumers	–	–	–	–	–	–	–	–

Source: Primary data from the rabbit entrepreneurs.

TABLE 7.6 : Channels of marketing of Rabbit wool on all farms in different districts of Himachal Pradesh

(Percentage)

No.	Channel Number	Channel	Districts							
			Chamba	*Hamirpur*	*Kangra*	*Kinnaur*	*Kullu*	*Mandi*	*Shimla*	*Solan*
1.	I	Producer-Wool Federation	52.66	40.00	56.25	–	19.23	21.95	66.67	40.01
2.	II	Producer-Hosiery-Consumer	5.26	–	–	–	7.69	19.51	–	18.18
3.	III	Producer-Hosiery-Wholesalers	–	–	–	–	–	–	–	–
4.	IV	Producer-Large Producers	10.52	20.00	6.25	40.00	7.69	21.95	33.33	23.63
5.	V	Producer-Traders Hosiery	10.52	40.00	25.00	60.00	26.92	14.63	–	14.54
6.	VI	Producer-Trader-Rabbit Yarn Factory	–	–	–	–	34.62	17.08	–	–
7.	VII	Producer-Self Processing-Consumers	21.04	–	12.50	–	3.85	4.88	–	3.64
8.	VIII	Producer-Processing-Commission Agent-Consumers	–	–	–	–	–	–	–	–

Source: Primary data from the rabbit entrepreneurs.

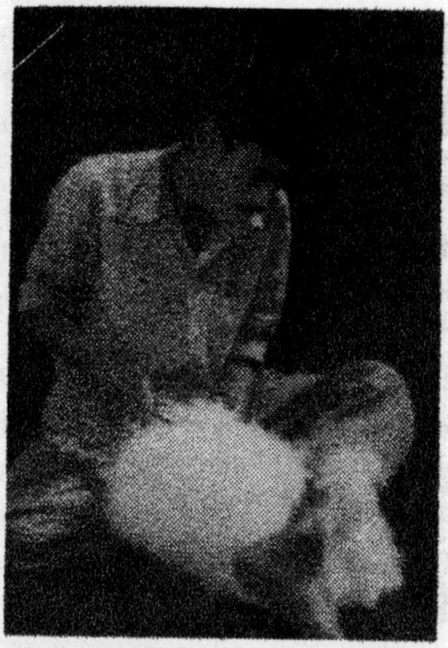

FIG. 8 : Wool shearing in progress

FIG. 9 : Newly born kits in a kindling box

The marketing costs incurred on small farms revealed that the transportation charges in all districts formed the major component of costs. The next highest charges were on shearing of rabbit wool.

On medium farms the transportation charges constituted the main component of marketing cost and in different districts it ranged between about 31 to 37 per cent of total marketing cost.

On large farms, the transportation charges are still higher and ranged between about 44 to 46 per cent. The higher charges are because of the hiring of public vehicles for transportation of wool from the farm to point of sale. The shearing charges were the next highest component of costs and ranged between about 14 to 18 per cent in different districts.

The costs incurred on marketing on all farms in different districts of Himachal Pradesh are presented in Table 7.10. The net price *i.e.* price after excluding marketing cost ranged between Rs. 705 in Chamba district to Rs. 722 in Mandi district of Himachal Pradesh. Among marketing costs the cost of transportation was the major component and accounted for 29.77 per cent in Solan district to 50.10 per cent in Chamba district. The next highest component in marketing cost was that of shearing charges which ranged between 19.05 per cent in Shimla to 25.06 per cent in Kinnaur district of Himachal Pradesh.

In a nutshell, the study of marketing channels and marketing costs on rabbit farms in different districts of Himachal Pradesh revealed that the main marketing channel on rabbit farms was Producer → Himachal Pradesh State Wool Federation and the main component of marketing cost was the cost of transportation of wool from the farm to the point of sale.

TABLE 7.7 : **Marketing costs on small rabbit farms in different districts of Himachal Pradesh**

(Rs/kg)

No.	Particulars	Districts							
		Chamba	*Hamirpur*	*Kangra*	*Kinnaur*	*Kullu*	*Mandi*	*Shimla*	*Solan*
A.	Gross Price Received	755	–	748	742	750	760	751	750
B.	Costs Incurred								
	i) Shearing charges	8.50 (16.95)	–	7.80 (22.77)	10.30 (25.05)	8.40 (21.79)	8.51 (20.01)	7.50 (19.05)	7.42 (19.76)
	ii) Packing material	2.10 (4.19)	–	2.55 (7.44)	2.14 (5.20)	2.48 (6.43)	2.50 (5.87)	2.72 (6.91)	2.85 (7.59)
	iii) Grading charges	6.20 (12.36)	–	5.12 (14.95)	4.31 (10.48)	6.36 (16.51)	5.91 (13.91)	5.68 (14.43)	5.43 (14.46)
	iv) Loading/unloading charges	3.12 (6.22)	–	2.30 (6.72)	3.25 (7.91)	4.12 (10.69)	3.98 (9.36)	4.02 (10.21)	4.15 (11.06)
	v) Transportation charges	25.12 (50.10)	–	12.30 (35.92)	16.40 (39.88)	13.20 (34.25)	16.44 (38.66)	12.34 (31.35)	11.45 (30.49)
	vi) Spoilage and losses	5.10 (10.18)	–	4.18 (12.20)	4.72 (11.48)	3.98 (10.33)	5.18 (12.19)	7.10 (18.05)	6.25 (16.64)
C.	Total Cost Incurred	50.14 (100.00)	–	34.25 (100)	41.12 (100)	38.54 (100)	42.52 (100)	39.36 (100)	37.55 (100)
D.	Net Price Received	705	–	714	701	711	717	712	712

Note : 1. Figures of net price received are rounded off.
2. Figures in parentheses indicate percentage to total cost.

Source: Primary data from the rabbit entrepreneurs.

TABLE 7.8 : Marketing costs on medium rabbit farms in different districts of Himachal Pradesh

(Rs/kg)

No.	Particulars	Districts							
		Chamba	*Hamirpur*	*Kangra*	*Kinnaur*	*Kullu*	*Mandi*	*Shimla*	*Solan*
A.	Gross Price Received	–	–	745	–	748	758	–	748
B.	Costs Incurred								
	i) Shearing charges	–	–	6.40	–	7.45	7.92	–	7.23
			(19.31)		(20.92)	(20.39)		(20.34)	
	ii) Packing material	–	–	2.32	–	2.15	2.40	–	2.16
			(7.00)		(6.03)	(6.16)		(6.08)	
	iii) Grading charges	–	–	5.00	–	5.98	5.10	–	5.22
			(15.09)		(16.78)	(13.10)		(14.68)	
	iv) Loading/unloading charges	–	–	2.12	–	4.00	3.92	–	4.11
				(6.40)		(11.23)	(10.01)		(11.56)
	v) Transportation charges	–	–	12.10	–	12.90	14.50	–	10.90
			(36.51)		(36.20)	(37.24)		(30.66)	
	vi) Spoilage & losses	–	–	5.20	–	3.15	5.10	–	5.93
			(15.69)		(8.84)	(13.10)		(16.68)	
C.	Total Cost Incurred	–	–	33.14	–	35.63	38.94	–	35.55
				(100)		(100)	(100)		(100)
D.	Net Price Received	–	–	712	–	712	719	–	712

Note : 1. Figures of net price received are rounded off.
2. Figures in parentheses indicate percentage to total cost.

Source: Primary data from the rabbit entrepreneurs.

TABLE 7 9 : Marketing costs on large rabbit farms in different districts of Himachal Pradesh

(Rs/kg)

No.	Particulars	Districts							
		Chamba	*Hamirpur*	*Kangra*	*Kinnaur*	*Kullu*	*Mandi*	*Shimla*	*Solan*
A.	Gross Price Received	–	756	745	–	748	760	–	–
B.	Costs Incurred								
	i) Shearing charges	–	4.90	6.10	–	7.10	7.51	–	–
		(14.05)	(17.54)		(18.08)	(17.68)			
	ii) Packing material	–	2.43	2.18	–	2.10	2.15	–	–
		(6.97)	(6.27)		(5.36)	(5.06)			
	iii) Grading charges	–	5.10	4.15	–	5.56	5.02	–	–
		(14.62)	(11.93)		(14.16)	(11.82)			
	iv) Loading/unloading charges	–	2.18	2.01	–	3.50	3.35	–	–
			(6.25)	(5.78)		(8.91)	(7.89)		
	v) Transportation charges	–	16.15	15.44	–	17.90	19.52	–	–
		(46.30)	(44.39)		(45.59)	(45.95)			
	vi) Spoilage and losses	–	4.12	4.90	–	3.10	4.93	–	–
			(11.81)	(14.09)		(7.90)	(11.60)		
C.	Total Cost Incurred	–	34.88	34.78	–	39.26	42.48	–	–
			(100)	(100)		(100)	(100)		
D.	Net Price Received	–	721	710	–	709	718	–	–

Note : 1. Figures of net price received are rounded off.
2. Figures in parentheses indicate percentage to total cost.

Source: Primary data from the rabbit entrepreneurs.

TABLE 7.10 : Marketing costs on all rabbit farms in different districts of Himachal Pradesh

(Rs/kg)

No.	Particulars	Districts							
		Chamba	*Hamirpur*	*Kangra*	*Kinnaur*	*Kullu*	*Mandi*	*Shimla*	*Solan*
A.	Gross Price Received	755	756	746	742	749	758	751	749
B.	Costs Incurred								
	i) Shearing charges	8.50	4.90	6.38	10.30	7.41	7.80	7.50	7.20
		(16.96)	(14.05)	(19.45)	(25.06)	(21.09)	(21.49)	(19.05)	(20.61)
	ii) Packing material	2.10	2.43	2.31	2.14	2.14	2.38	2.72	2.14
		(4.19)	(6.97)	(7.04)	(5.20)	(6.09)	(6.56)	(6.91)	(6.13)
	iii) Grading charges	6.20	5.10	5.01	4.31	5.97	5.05	5.68	5.20
		(12.36)	(14.62)	(15.28)	(10.48)	(16.99)	(13.91)	(14.43)	(14.89)
	iv) Loading/unloading charges	3.12	2.18	2.10	3.25	3.98	3.91	4.02	4.10
		(6.22)	(6.25)	(6.40)	(7.90)	(11.32)	(10.77)	(10.21)	(11.74)
	v) Transportation charges	25.12	16.15	11.90	16.40	12.52	12.10	12.34	10.40
		(50.10)	(46.30)	(36.28)	(39.88)	(35.63)	(33.34)	(31.15)	(29.77)
	vi) Spoilage and losses	5.10	4.12	5.10	4.72	3.12	5.05	7.10	5.89
		(10.17)	(11.81)	(15.55)	(11.48)	(8.88)	(13.91)	(18.04)	(16.86)
C.	Total Cost Incurred	50.14	34.88	32.80	41.12	35.14	36.29	39.36	34.93
		(100)	(100)	(100)	(100)	(100)	(100)	(100)	(100)
D.	Net Price Received	705	721	713	701	714	722	712	714

Note: 1. Figures of net price received are rounded off.
2. Figures in parentheses indicate percentage to total cost.

Source: Primary data from the rabbit entrepreneurs.

8

PACKAGE OF PRACTICES AND TECHNOLOGICAL GAP

8.1 Selection of Site

Important considerations to be made while selecting a site for establishing a rabbitry are:

i) Protection from extreme weather conditions like direct sunlight, noise etc., which can interfere with the performance and comfort of rabbits.

ii) Protection from predators, snakes, insects etc.

iii) Sloppy land is better suited to avoid water logging and sheds should be constructed at higher plane than ground level. The sheds should not face towards windward direction.

iv) Economic and marketing considerations are very important while planning the rabbitry and for controlling cost and maximizing profits from rabbit production :

a) Efficient and cheap labour should be available in the surrounding areas.

b) Locally available building materials should preferably be utilized while constructing new buildings. Existing buildings and structures like poultry sheds can be suitably modified to save expenses on new constructions.

v) The type of floor, earth or concrete depends upon building and its location. To reduce ammonia concentration, exits should be provided for immediate drainage of urine but this is not needed with open sheds, *kutcha* floors and arid climates. The excreta removal can be either done mechanically or by flushing, the former is preferred to reduce humidity.

vi) The building should be able to provide good heat insulation in temperate environment and adequate protection from heat in tropical and sub-tropical climatic conditions. In closed sheds more ventilation is to be provided.

8.2 Temperature Requirement

Though the rabbits can be maintained from –2°C to 35°C but the optimum environmental temperature is 15–25°C.

8.3 Humidity

The ideal humidity of an indoor rabbitry is about 75 per cent at a temperature of about 60°F.

8.4 Air Quality and Ventilation

The rabbit is much more sensitive to air quality (relative humidity, concentration of noxious gases and movement of air) than to temperature. So proper ventilation of the rabbitry is also essential. Inadequate ventilation leads to smell of ammonia, condensation temperature or relative humidity compared with the outside air and a marked differences in the temperatures recorded by a maximum-minimum thermometer.

8.5 Light

Normally 16 hours light and 8 hours dark pattern should be used. Not only the light pattern be correct but the intensity of light should be at a suitable level. For a continual production of young throughout the year, a constant duration of light from 12–16 hours per day, is therefore, recommended. Angora rabbits for wool production should be given 16-9 hours decreasing duration of lighting in the course of the shearing interval. Artificial light of 20 lux are sufficient.

A white fluorescent light will give 25 lux at 2 meters below the fitting if used at the rate of 0.7 to 1 watt per square meter. Two 40 watt tubes per 10 sq m (100 ft sq) would provide this amount of illumination satisfactorily.

8.6 Size of Cages

The size of cages for different category of rabbits is given in Table 8.1.

TABLE 8.1 : Size of cages for different categories of rabbits

No.	*Rabbit category*	*Surface (sqm)*	*Measurements (cm)*		
			Width	*Length*	*Height*
1.	Breeding animals (up to 4 kg live weight)	0.2	40	50	30
2.	Breeding animals (up to 5.5 kg live weight)	0.3	50	60	35
3.	Breeding animals (above 5.5 kg)	0.4	55	75	40
4.	Fattening rabbits (2.7 kg live weight in groups)	Upto 0.08	–	–	–
5.	Angora rabbits (wool production)	0.2	40	50	35

8.7 Feeding Fixtures

When choosing feeders, consistencies of feed (concentrate, mash or pellets) or roughage (green forage, silage, hay etc.) should be considered.

Automatic feeders of plastic or galvanized tin consisting of storage container (capacity up to 3 kg) out of which the pellets will slide into a trough. The upper rim of the trough should have 15-20 mm bend towards the inner side to prevent losses of feed. Round automatic feeders as used in poultry can also be used for group feeding. The feeding space required for medium heavy animals (upto 4 kg live weight) should be at least 8 cm/animals with long troughs and 6 cm/animal with round troughs. Feeding hoppers of galvanised wire, meal rods, plastic rods or bamboo etc., are suitable for feeding roughages. They should be large enough to hold half of its daily requirements.

8.8 Watering fixtures

Inverted water bottle fitted into a small trough (small enough to prevent contamination) can make good waterer for small rabbitry. In large units, automatic drinkers (nipple drinkers or suckling drinkers) fitted with centrally servicing tank is best suited to supply clean uncontaminated water in each cage.

8.9 Nest Box

The nest boxes are one of the most important equipments in rabbit production for reducing mortality in pre-weaning stage. Nest boxes can be constructed of galvanized iron, wood or wire mesh. The entrance to box should be at least 16–18 cm^2 or round and be fixed at least 7-10 cm above the box floor. It should be possible to close the entrance by sliding device. The bottom of the box should be so designed to allow easy draining of urine. The bottom should be hollow. The minimum measurements of nesting boxes are given in Table 8.2

TABLE 8.2 : Measurements of nesting boxes

Particulars	*Measurements (cm)*		
	Width	*Depth*	*Height*
Doe up to 4.0 kg	33	33	25
Doe above 4.0 kg	30	40	30

8.10 Management of Rabbits

Quality management increases income, reduces cost of production and produces competitive quality product. The management includes following parameters :

8.10.1 Production Cycle

Under most intensive system of rabbit production, as followed by the European breeders (France, Italy, Spain etc.), the does attain maturity at 4-5 months of age. Subsequent matings are done within 48 h of kindling and weaning advanced to 24–28 days. But this requires very high Management skill and high plane of nutrition and hence seldom recommended for new rabbit raisers.

It is the semi-intensive system which is best suited for conditions in developing countries. In this, the does are first mated at 5-6 months of age and subsequent matings after 10-12 days of kindling. Weaning is usually done at 28 to 40 days of age.

Extensive system is not followed on commercial scale production, it has long interval between kindling and subsequent matings and weaning is also done at about 56 days.

8.10.2 Mating

Mating is invariable done in buck's cage. Pinkish-red vulva is an important sign of doe in heat in which there are 80-90% chances of successful mating as compared to dry pale vulva (10-20% chances of success). After successful service, the buck usually falls to his side and the doe is removed to her cage. It takes hardly 5 minutes for service. If the doe refuses to mate, it can be presented to another buck by postponing the mating for a day. Conception rates under forces matings are usually less than that of normal unrestrained matings. Other signs of doe being in heat are behaving restlessly, rubbing the chin on cage, making an effort to join other rabbits in adjoining cages. Artificial insemination with hormonal injection 2-4 hr after insemination can be successfully used to reduce the number of breeding bucks being maintained.

8.10.3 Number of Bucks

One buck can serve 7-8 does in intensive system 10-15 in extensive system but should not be used more than 3-4 days in a week. Usually a unit of 10+2 is recommended to start with.

8.10.4 Age to Breed

The mating of medium sized does can be done at 4-5 months of age and bucks at about 5 months of age can be used for service of they have attained 80% of the adult live weight.

8.10.5 Pregnancy Diagnosis

Abdomen palpation after 14 days of mating is a reliable method to diagnose pregnant does. It is not effective before 9 days and after 14th day, as there are chances of abortion. If the doe is found empty, it can be re-mated immediately.

8.10.6 Gestation Period

Average gestation period in does is 31 days and 98% of kindling takes place between 30th to 33rd day after mating.

8.10.7 Kindling

Kindling should be allowed to take place quietly and in hygienic surroundings. The nest should be checked immediately after kindling and dead litter be removed. The nest box containing bedding material should be placed in the cage 28 days after mating. The doe will make a nest of straw etc., and remove fur from hip, dewlap or mammary region to complete the nest.

The period between birth and weaning is most important for the successful rearing of rabbits. Even in European countries mortality rate of 20 per cent is normal during this period. The major causes being the managemental problems (improper equipments , failure to nurse by doe, dropping of litter or cage or nest box, presence of strangers or predators during kindling), cannibalism, still birth and delayed birth infections (salmonellosis, pasteurellosis and listeriosis). Rearing losses increase with increased litter size.

8.10.8 Fostering

The litter size varies between 1-24 but the most common is 7-8 for medium heavy breeds. If the litter is large and unmanageable, the breeders may separate them into smaller litters by giving to foster mothers. Fostering is done within 5 days of kindling and the young ones for about 5 minute in 24 hours mainly during morning hours. The number of teats is usually 8 and seldom 10-12. Surplus young ones have little chances of obtaining milk. Synchronised kindling helps in reducing losses by equalization of litter through fostering.

8.10.9 Weaning

Weaning is done at 28-40 days when the approximate kit weight is 500 g. The young rabbits start eating solid food at 18 to 20 days and by 30th day the milk constitutes hardly 20 per cent of the total feed intake. All the kits are weaned simultaneously. If rabbits are to be kept beyond 3 months, the bucks must be either put in individual cages or castrated. The females may be allowed to remain in single cage.

8.10.10 Sexing

Sexing is usually done at the time of weaning but a trained person can perform sexing at 2 to 3 days after kindling by pressing observing the sexual organs. This helps in maintaining bucks and does separately for breeding purposes.

8.10.11 Handling of Rabbits

The rabbits are always lifted by grasping fold of skin over the shoulder with one hand and placing the other hand below rump to support the weight of animal. If the animal struggles, it is better to drop it and then to pick up afresh correctly. Never to be lifted by ears or legs. For carrying rabbits to some distance, hold it against your body with its head under one arm, holding the skin fold of shoulder region.

8.10.12 Identification

Individual or cage identification can be done for economic management of rabbitry. Individual identification can be done by ear-clipping or tattooing or by ear tags.

In intensive production system rapid replacement of breeding stock is desired (monthly culling rates 8-10%) for improvement in the quality and health of the stock. In general save one replacement doe per month for every 12 breeding does and one buck for every 5 breeding bucks. Selection is the common method of renewing the breeding stock. To avoid inbreeding, bucks and sometimes the does are to be procured from other breeders.

8.10.13 Technical Records

Different type of records to be maintained include the pedigree sheet of each animal, cage record card, buck breeding record, doe breeding card, stock register, feed register, fattening record, growth register, wool record (Angora) and weekly work plan etc. Such records will be of immense help in selecting and culling the animals and for determining the profit and loss of the enterprise.

8.10.14 Feed Stuffs

The recommended nutrient content in complete feed stuffs for Angora rabbits (weight per kg diet) is given in Table 8.3.

TABLE 8.3 : Recommended nutrient contents in complete feed*

	Fattening	*Breeding*	*Wool Production*
DE Kcal	2900	2600	2200–2600
CP %	16–18	15–17	15–17
EE %	16–18	15–17	15–17
CF %	7–10	10–14	14–16
Amino Acids			
Lysine %	1.0	1.0	0.5
Methinonine and cystine. %	0.4–0.6	0.7	0.7
Arginine %	0–6	0.6	0.6

Note : DE: Digestible energy, CP: Crude protein, CF: Crude fibre, EE: Ether extract.

*After Schlolant (1984).

8.10.15 Energy Requirement

The average daily digestible energy for maintenance and production can be estimated by the formula given by Church, D.C., 1991*.

---

* Church, D.C. (1991), *Livestock Feeds and Feeding.* Third edition. Prentice - Hall, Germany.

DE = 4 MV (20-WW) + 55 WW + 3.6 DG - 50

Whereas for lactating animals the formula is DE = 290 + 65 DW + 35 G

Where,

DE = digestible energy (K cal/day)

MW= estimated market weight (kg)

WW= Weaning weight (kg)

DG = expected average daily gain (g)

DW = doe weight (kg)

G = number of suckling rabbits.

8.10.16 Illustration

For a rabbit that is going to be marketed at 2 kg, with a weaning weight of 0.6 kg and an expected daily gain of 30 g, the estimated DE requirement per day for the growing period would be

$$4 \times 2\,(20-0.6) + 55\,(0.6) + 3.6\,(30) - 50 = 246.2 \text{ K cal}$$

If the feed utilized 2500 K cal DE/kg then feed consumption/animal/day (waste not included) will be

$$\frac{246.2 \times 1000}{2500} = 98.48 \text{ g of feed}$$

8.11 Technological Gap

The technological gap on all farms has been given in Table 8.2. The study revealed that the maximum technological gap of 17.80 per cent existed in case of feed followed by size of cages (16.78%) and light (15.62%). The maximum technological gap in feed is attributed to high prices of the feed since the returns being low due to low price of the wool farmers are unable to provide recommended quantity of feed. The farmers substituted fodder for feed, therefore, the quantity of fodder fed is higher than the recommended quantity. The negative technological gap showed that these inputs are being used in a more quantity than the recommended doses. The maximum negative technological gap existed in case of medication (-171.8%) followed by roughages (-89.91%) and labour (-69.47%). The negative technological gap in medication showed the over use of the medicines and money spent on it. This is attributed to the small number of rabbits on farms and packing of medicines is such that it is meant for larger flock. Since small packings are not available, therefore, farmers have to spend much money, however, the medicines remains unutilized because of larger packing. The next lowest negative technological gap in roughages is attributed to substitution of roughages for fodder. The over utilization of labour is because of small size of farms as economies of scale in performing various operations are not achieved.

TABLE 8.4 : Technological gap on all rabbit farms

No.	*Particulars*	*Unit*	*Recommended Technology*	*Existing situation*	*Technological Gap (%)*
1.	Feed	Kg	5110	4200.18	17.80
2.	Roughages	Kg	3650	6931.78	-89.91
3.	Medication	Rs	500	1359	-171.8
4.	Labour	Mandays	183	310.14	-69.47
5.	Cage size	Cu cm	16,8000 (70x60x40)	139806 (56.5x58.8x36.3)	16.78
6.	Breeding box	Cu cm	23750	22667	4.56
7.	Light	Hours	16	13.5	15.62
8.	Shearing interval	Months	3.00	3.10	-3.33
9.	Weaning	Weeks	5.00	4.80	4.00
10.	Wool yield	Kg	75.00	52.43	30.09

Source: Primary data from the rabbit entrepreneurs.

9

PROBLEMS AND CONSTRAINTS EXPERIENCED BY RABBIT ENTREPRENEURS

This Chapter depicts the various problems and constraints experienced by rabbit entrepreneurs in Himachal Pradesh. The problems faced by rabbit entrepreneurs have been categorised into four subheads viz; production, financial, marketing and institutional problems. The rabbit entrepreneurs were interviewed in respect of various problems and their per cent response has been given in various sub-heads. The difference in the extent of problems faced by small, medium, large and overall category of farmers has also been tested by employing Chi-square distribution.The null-hypothesis (H^0: = $p'1 = p'2 = p'3 = p'4$) *i.e.*, the extent of problems is same in all the categories of rabbit entrepreneurs was tested. The calculated value (k^2 = 411.65) of Chi-square was greater than the table value (k^2 = 112.33). Therefore, it led to the rejectionof null-hypothesis, *i.e.* hypothesis of no difference and revealed that the problems differ significantly in different categories of entrepreneurs and they can be reduced if proper management practices are adopted by rabbit entrepreneurs and requires different way of tackling for each category.

Jithendran (1998) studied the different constraints faced by the farmers in rabbit rearing and revealed that compared to other farm livestock and poultry, rabbit production is more demanding of technical knowledge and care. Due to the less production performance at high temperature rabbit production is less suitable for hot humid tropics. Feed is expensive and is the major cost of production. Lack of proper marketing of rabbit meat, fur and wool is also a major constraint faced by the farmer.

9.1 Production Problems of Rabbit Entrepreneurs

The production problems of rabbit entrepreneurs had been further sub-categorised into twelve types viz., availability of feed, price of feed, shortage of fodder, availability of cages, feeders, waterers, process of equipments, problem of pests and diseases, availability of veterinary aid, availability of medicine, availability of labour, high labour wages, availability of fresh blood (breeding animals to avoid inbreeding), maintenance of financial and pedigree records. The different production problems confronted by wool rabbitry entrepreneurs are given in Table 9.1.

9.1.1 Non-availability of feed at appropriate time

The availability of quality feed is an important component in rabbit production. About 52 per cent of rabbit entrepreneurs reported that the feed was not available at right time. The quality of the feed is also very important. The rabbit entrepreneurs reported that the sub-standard feed led to deaths *en-masse* and heavy losses to them.

The perusal of the table reveals that the gravity of the problem and farm size has an inverse relationship the gravity decreased with the increase in farm size.

9.1.2 High prices of feed

The feed prices when compared to output prices are quite high. About 72 per cent of the rabbit entrepreneurs on overall farms reported this problem and the gravity of the problem and farm size showed inverse relationship. The per cent response decreased with increase in farm size. About 95 per cent of small farms revealed the high prices of feed whereas, the per cent response on all large farms was about 35 per cent only.

9.1.3 Scarcity of fodder

The commonly fed fodder in the study area are common grasses, bamboo leaves, barseem, biul (*Grewia robusta* and *Grewia optiva*) leaves and kitchen waste. About 12 per cent of the rabbit entrepreneurs reported acute shortage of fodder in the study area. The shortage of fodder is experienced during winter. The maximum shortage of fodder was experienced on medium farms (15.56%) followed by small and large farms.

9.1.4 Non-availability of cages, feeders and waterers

About 18 per cent of the entrepreneurs reported that the inputs like cages, feeders and waterers are not available. The tally was highest for large farms 35.48 per cent followed by medium farm (28.89%) and small farms 6.45 per cent. The extent of problem increased with the increase in farm size hence showed positive correlation between gravity of problem and farm size.

9.1.5 High prices of cages, feeders and waterers

The problem of high prices of cages, feeders and waterers showed a positive correlation with the size of the farm. About 24 per cent of rabbit entrepreneurs on all farms reported the problems of high prices of these equipments. Since large rabbit entrepreneurs buy these equipments in bulk and experience more problem.

9.1.6 Problem of pests and diseases

The problem of pest and diseases was depicted by about 9 per cent of entrepreneurs on all farms and the per cent response increased with the increase in farm size.

9.1.7 Veterinary aid not available when required

About 22 per cent of rabbit entrepreneurs confronted this problem on all farms category of rabbit entrepreneurs. The gravity of non-availability of veterinary aid and farm size showed positive correlation. The maximum response of 45.16 per cent was reported on large farms followed by 35.56 per cent on medium farms and 7.53 per cent on small farms.

9.1.8 Non-availability of medicines

The non-availability of medicines was reported to the extent of about 11 per cent on all farms. The maximum per cent response

TABLE 9.1 : Production problems of the rabbit entrepreneurs

(Per cent)

No.	Particulars	Farm Size			
		Small	Medium	Large	All Farms
1.	Quality feed not available at appropriate time	72.04	35.56	16.13	52.07
2.	Feed prices not reasonable	94.62	51.11	35.48	72.19
3.	Shortage of fodder	11.83	15.56	9.68	12.43
4.	Cages, feeders and waterers not available at right time	6.45	28.89	35.48	17.75
5.	Price of cages, feeders and waterers are high.	7.53	37.78	54.84	24.26
6.	Problem of pest and diseases	1.08	11.11	29.03	8.88
7.	Veterinary aid not available when required	7.53	35.56	45.16	21.89
8.	Medicines not available at right time	6.45	24.44	6.45	11.24
9.	Labour not available when required	58.06	22.22	16.13	40.83
10.	Labour charges not reasonable	37.63	26.66	25.81	31.95
11.	Non-availability of fresh blood.	38.71	31.11	9.68	31.36
12.	Non maintenance of financial and pedigree records	97.85	71.11	74.19	86.39
	Total number of farms	**93**	**45**	**31**	**169**

Note: Figures have been rounded off to their nearest digit.

Source: Primary data from the rabbit entrepreneurs.

was recorded on medium farms 24.44 per cent. However, it was a tie (6.45%) on small and large farms.

9.1.9 Non-availability of Labour

The non-availability of labour was experienced by about 41 per cent on all farms category. The gravity of the problem of non-availability of labour and farm size showed an inverse relationship. The response was maximum on small farms (58.06%) followed by medium farms 22.22 per cent on medium farms and

16.13 per cent on large farms. The large farms have created employment for labourers.

9.1.10 High Wages of Labour

The high wages of labour for attending rabbits was experienced by about 32 per cent of entrepreneurs on all farms category. The extent of the problem decreased with increase in size and thereby showing an inverse relationship between extent of problem and farm size. The response recorded was as high as 37.63 per cent on small farms followed by 26.66 per cent on medium farms and 25.81 per cent on large farms.

9.1.11 Non-Availability of Fresh-Blood

The inbreeding in rabbits leads to decreased output, high incidence of diseases and mortality among the flock. Therefore, introduction of fresh blood of pure strain at frequent intervals is very important to eliminate the adverse consequences of inbreeding in a rabbitry. About 31 per cent of rabbit entrepreneurs on all farms reported the problem of non-availability of fresh blood. The gravity of the problem was maximum on small farms (38.71%) followed by medium farms 31.11 per cent and 9.68 per cent on large farms thereby depicting inverse relationship between extent of problem and farm size.

9.1.12 Maintenance of Financial and Pedigree Records

The problem of maintaining financial and pedigree records was as high as about 86 per cent on all farms. The maximum response was recorded on small farms 97.85 per cent followed by large farms 74.19 per cent and medium farms 71.11 per cent.

9.2. Financial Problems of Rabbit Entrepreneurs

The establishment of rabbitry units require some capital investment in the beginning. The finance is needed to construct shed, purchase cages, waterers, feederers and purchase of the breeding stock. The banks have a scheme to finance small and marginal farmers or agricultural labourers for small units size of 10 female + 2 male. However, if large entrepreneurs are interested to take up the scheme they could be financed for more than one unit depending upon individual needs and merits of each case.

The banks also make provision for providing veterinary aid, fodder and concentrated feed and training of beneficiaries. The loan limit is Rs. 2430 for a unit of 10 females + 2 males for fur/meat and Rs. 8850 for a unit of wool type breeding rabbits. Considering larger loan required for the latter unit, it is necessary that beneficiaries with adequate resources and experience are selected. The disbursement of loan is against purchase of equipments and breeding animals on the supply of bills of such items. The initial recurring expenses for first 6 months for pelleted feed have been capitalized term loan. The disbursement against supply of feed is also done against bills of supply. The loan against breeding animals is disbursed only when equipment and initial stock of one month feed is purchased and inexperienced farmer receives adequate training. Margin money by beneficiaries at the rate of 15 to 25 per cent for wool unit as per ARDC norms is envisaged. The rate of interest to ultimate borrowers will depend upon the amount of loan raised. However, the rate of interest varies from 12 per cent to 23.75 per cent with quarterly or half yearly interests. The security against the loan is hypothecation of rabbits, feed, fodder, equipment fixtures and other movable created out of the bank loan. Secondly, creation of equitable mortgage/charge over applicants land where sheds are constructed and thirdly, third party guarantee of sufficient worth good for loan amount.

The supervision of the credit is through regular visits to the unit in order to ensure proper utilization of loan amount disbursed for construction of sheds, purchase of equipments and rabbit stock. Thereafter, monthly inspections will be carried out regularly when the project commences.

The bank also makes a provision for adequate and comprehensive insurance cover in respect of shed equipment against fire, theft, earthquake, riots and rabbit mortality during the period of loan and relevant policies are also arranged in favour of bank. Banks assume that daily requirements of about two hours per unit for adult rabbits and the progeny, scheme would provide additional employment of 90 days per year per unit.

The contact with the farmers through survey revealed that majority of the farmers are not aware of the loan facility. The financial

TABLE 9.2 : Financial problems of the rabbit entrepreneurs

(Per cent)

No.	Particulars	Farm Size			All Farms
		Small	Medium	Large	
1.	Credit not abailable at appropriate time	93.55	86.67	96.77	92.31
2.	Credit given not supervised	95.70	93.33	96.77	95.27
3.	Available credit is inadequate	93.55	86.67	96.77	92.31
	Total number of farms	**93**	**45**	**31**	**169**

Note: Figures have been rounded off to their nearest digit.
Source: Primary data from the rabbit entrepreneurs.

problems confronted by rabbit entrepreneurs have been presented in Table 9.2.

9.2.1 Non-availability of Credit at Appropriate Time

The non-availability of credit at appropriate time was reported by 92.31 per cent of rabbit entrepreneurs on all farms situation. The maximum response to this problem was recorded on large farms 96.77 per cent followed by small farms 93.55 per cent and medium farms 86.67 per cent.

Since the rabbit industry in Himachal Pradesh is in recession and banks advance loans only to those entrepreneurs whose risk bearing ability and repayment capacity is high. Small rabbit entrepreneurs do not gather courage to have loan under present circumstances when rabbit industry is passing through a slump.

9.2.2 No Supervision of Credit

About 95 per cent of rabbit entrepreneurs on all farms situations reported that credit once given is not properly supervised. The response recorded was maximum on large farms (96.77%) followed by small and medium rabbit entrepreneurs respectively.

9.2.3 Inadequate Credit

The rabbit entrepreneurs reported that credit given is not adequate 92.31 per cent of rabbit entrepreneurs on all farms reported that available credit was inadequate. Among different size of rabbit entrepreneurs, the maximum response was recorded on large farms and it was to the tune of 96.77 per cent followed by small farms 93.55 per cent and 86.67 per cent on medium farms.

9.3 Marketing Problems

The availability of proper marketing facilities is a prerequisite for the development of any enterprise. An efficient marketing system for the disposal of farm produce leads to faster growth and development. The profitability also depends on the factors like location of market, storage, transportation facilities and grading of farm products. So far there is no stable and organized market for Angora rabbit farming on large scale. There is a demand for better breeds of Angoras but the sale/disposal of ordinary surplus animals is not organized and ensured. The various marketing problems noticed on farms are given in Table 9.3.

9.3.1 Inadequate Transportation Facilities

Transportation plays an important role in the marketing of produce which has to be shifted from the point of production to the point of final consumption. Comparatively the problem of transportation of the inputs and produce was revealed by a less number of rabbit entrepreneurs. On all farms situation only 11.24 per cent of entrepreneurs reported this problem. Maximum response in favour of inadequate transportation was recorded on large farms (45.16%) followed by medium farms (11.11%). However, the problem of transportation was not confronted on small farms.

9.3.2 Insufficient Market

Rabbitry entrepreneurs in the study area reported to have insufficient market system. There were no ready buyers of rabbit products, especially wool, locally, so the farmers had either to transport it to distant towns or sell in the local market at low premium. About 40 per cent of the farmers on all farms situation responded to this problem.

TABLE 9.3 : Marketing problems of the rabbit entrepreneurs

(Per cent)

No.	Particulars	Farm Size			All Farms
		Small	Medium	Large	
1.	Inadequate Transportation Facilities	–	11.11	45.16	11.24
2.	Regular markets for farm product	37.63	37.78	51.61	40.24
3.	Unremunerative price of meat	100.00	100.00	100.00	100.00
4.	Unremunerative price of wool	100.00	100.00	100.00	100.00
5.	Problem of grading costs	29.03	2.22	9.68	18.34
6.	High marketing costs	10.75	31.11	61.29	24.26
7.	Support price by government should be fixed	43.01	62.22	77.42	54.44
8.	Price of breeder rabbits not remunerative	98.92	73.33	77.42	88.17
9.	Demand of wool products seasonal	100.00	95.56	100.00	98.82
	Total number of farms	**93**	**45**	**31**	**169**

Note : Figures have been rounded-off to their nearest digit.

Source: Primary data from the rabbit entrepreneurs.

9.3.3 Unremunerative Prices of Meat

The problem of unremunerative prices of meat was responded positively by each and every entrepreneur on all categories of farms. Rabbit meat could not be popularized among meat eaters in Himachal Pradesh.

However, rabbit meat has many desirable traits like low fat and cholesterol, high proteins and minerals. The wool rabbits when become uneconomical with the passage of age are sold at throw away prices. Therefore, 100 per cent of rabbit entrepreneurs in all the categories confronted this problem.

9.3.4 Unremunerative Prices of Wool

The problem of unremunerative prices of wool has been responded positively by each and every rabbit entrepreneur on all the categories of farms. With the liberalisation the access to market by developed nations has increased. The Government of India has reduced tariff on import of wool to a greater extent and as a result the rabbit wool was available at a cheaper rate than home produced. Therefore, in the recent past year the prices of wool have slashed and farmers are not getting remunerative prices for their produce.

9.3.5 Problem of Grading

The different grades of rabbit wool have different prices and traders cheat rabbit entrepreneurs by designating their produce as "B" grade wool. The problem of grading of wool before selling was revealed by 18.34 per cent of rabbit entrepreneurs on all farms situation. The maximum response was recorded on small farms which was to the extent of 29.03 per cent followed by large farms (9.68%) and medium farm 2.22 per cent.

9.3.6 High Marketing Costs

The marketing costs in rabbitry includes the cost of transportation, storage and other fees if any. High marketing costs were reported by 24.26 per cent of rabbit entrepreneurs on all farms situation. The problem of high marketing cost and size of the farm showed a positive correlation. The gravity of the problem of high marketing costs increased with the increase in farm size. On small farms 10.75 per cent of rabbit entrepreneurs responded to this problem. On medium farms (31.11%) and on large farms 61.29 per cent reported this problem.

9.3.7 Support Price of Rabbit Wool

About 54 per cent of rabbit entrepreneurs on all farms situation revealed that the government should fix support price for rabbit wool. The per cent response of the rabbit entrepreneur increased with the increase in size of a farm, 43.01 per cent of small farms, 62.22 per cent of medium farms and 77.42 per cent of large rabbit entrepreneurs revealed that government should fix the support price for rabbit wool.

9.3.8 Price of Rabbits Unremunerative

The rabbits are purchased for establishing new rabbit units and also for cross-breeding purpose. About 88 per cent of rabbit entrepreneur on all farms situation revealed that the existing price of the animals is not remunerative. The problem of unremunerative prices was reported by 98.92 per cent of entrepreneurs on small farms followed by large farms (77.42%) and medium farms (73.33%).

9.3.9 Seasonal Demand for Wool Products

The demand for rabbit wool and other products is seasonal. During winter the demand for wool products rises, whereas, it decreases in other months of the year. The seasonal demand for wool products was reported by 98.82 per cent on all farms. All the rabbit entrepreneurs on small and large farms reported the seasonal demand for wool.

9.4 Institutional Problems

The institutional problems faced by rabbit entrepreneurs have been studied under subheads like lack of training and extension facilities and availability of package of practices and presented in Table 9.4.

TABLE 9.4 : Institutional problems of the rabbit entrepreneurs

(Per cent)

No.	Particulars	Farm Size			All Farms
		Small	Medium	Large	
1.	Training Facilities not Adequate	12.90	51.11	32.26	26.63
2.	Lack of Extension Facilities	93.55	66.67	83.87	84.62
3.	Package of Practices not available	100.00	53.33	74.19	82.84
	Total number of farms	**93**	**45**	**31**	**169**

Note : Figures have been rounded-off to their nearest digit.
Source: Primary data from the rabbit entrepreneurs.

9.4.1 Inadequate Training Facilities

The rabbit rearing is an art as well as science and requires technical knowledge. The knowledge acquired through training is of great relevance. The different institutions organize training programmes for rabbit entrepreneurs. About 27 per cent of rabbit entrepreneurs on all farms situation reported that existing training facilities are not adequate. The maximum response in favour of this problem was found on medium farms (51.11%) followed by large farms (32.26%) and small farms (12.90 per cent).

9.4.2 Lack of Extension Facilities

The rabbit entrepreneurs expect time to time help and guidance from different agencies of government. 84.62 per cent of rabbit entrepreneurs on all farms reported the lack of extension facilities. However, the maximum response was recorded on small farms (93.55%) followed by large (83.87%) and medium farms (66.67%), respectively.

9.4.3 Non-availability of Package of Practices

The improved technology developed by research institutes is disseminated through package of practices. Eighty three per cent of rabbit entrepreneurs reported the non-availability of package of practices. Cent per cent response with regard to this problem was recorded on small farms. However, 53.33 per cent of medium farms and 74.19 per cent of large farms reported this problem respectively.

10

REGRESSION ANALYSIS

To examine the input-output relationship linear as well as Cobb-Douglas type of production functions were tried.

The Cobb-Douglas production function was tried because its regression co-efficients are the direct measures of elasticities of production with respect to individual input. The returns to scale are obtained directly summing the regression co-efficients. The computational work involved in fitting this function is simpler than others. The linear as well as Cobb-Douglas Production Function were fitted independently for districts having more than 30 observations. In some of the districts where observations were less, data for two or more districts were pooled. The production functions were fitted for small, medium and large farmers separately.

10.1 Linear Production Function

The linear production function of the following form was tried

$Y = a+b_1x_1+b_2x_2+b_3X_3+b_4x_4+b_5x_5$

Where,

Y = Rabbit wool production (kg/100 animals/year)

X_1 = Feed consumption (kg/100 rabbits/year)

X_2 = Fodder consumption (kg/100 rabbits/year)

X_3 = Value of medicines (Rs/100 rabbits/year)

X_4 = Labour employed (man days/100 rabbits/year)

X_5 = Working capital (Rs/100 rabbits/year)

b_1, b_2, b_3, b_4 and b_5 are regression co-efficients.

10.2 Cobb-Douglas Production Function

The Cobb-Douglas production function of the following form was employed :

$$Y = ax_1^{b1}x_2^{b2}x_3^{b3}x_4^{b4}x_5^{b5}x_6^{b6}e^u$$

The symbols have same meaning as explained in linear production function and e^u stands for error term.

10.2.1 Cobb-Douglas Production Function for Solan Farmers

The results of fitted Cobb-Douglas production function for Solan farmers have been presented in Table 10.1. The study of the table reveal that the regression co-efficients in respect of fodder and value of medicines were turned out to be significant. Whereas, regression co-efficients in respect of other independent variables feed, human labour and working capital were non-significant.

The regression co-efficient of fodder revealed that one per cent increase in fodder, on an average, will increase wool yield by 1.2229 per cent, keeping feed, medicines, human labour and working capital constant at their geometric mean levels. Similarly, the regression co-efficient in respect of value of medicines was negative and significant. Thereby, revealing that one per cent increase in expenditure on medicines will reduce the wool yield by 0.2030 per cent, keeping feed, fodder, human labour and working capital constant at their geometric mean levels. The value of R^2 was found to be significant at 5 per cent level of significance. The calculated value of F was 3.5408 and the table value was 2.45 at 5 and 40 degrees of freedom. Thereby, showing that the included independent variables are significantly expressing the variation in the wool yield.

The negative sign of regression co-efficient in case of medicines is attributed to over use of medicines. As small packing of some medicines was not available for small flock. So farmers had to buy a complete unit resulting in wastage of contents after use and increasing their expenses on medicines. The value of co-efficient of multiple determination was computed as 0.2736 revealing that the included independent variables feed, fodder, value of medicine, human labour and working capital only explained 27.36 per cent of variation in wool yield. However, the value of R^2 was significant at 5 per cent level of significance.

TABLE 10.1 : Cobb-douglas production function for small farmers in district Solan of Himachal Pradesh

No.	Particulars	Constant	Production Elasticities				
			Feed (x_1)	Fodder (x_2)	Medicines (x_3)	Human labour (x_4)	Working capital (x_5)
1.	Production function	–5.3089	–0.2367	1.2229*	–0.2030*	0.0773	0.1373
2.	Standard error	4.2535	0.1945	0.4590	0.0699	0.0799	0.1187
3.	t-value	1.2481	1.2167	2.6642	–2.9057	0.9677	1.1572
4.	R^2	0.2736*					
5.	$\bar{R}^2$	0.1963*					
6.	F-value	3.5408					
7.	Degrees of freedom	47					
8.	Regression sum of square	0.9568					
9.	Error sum of square	2.5400					

Source : Primary data from the rabbit farmers.

*Significant at 5 per cent level of significance.

The results of the fitted linear production function for small farmers of Solan district has been given in Appendix-II.

10.2.2 Cobb-Douglas production function for small rabbit entrepreneurs in Kullu, Kinnaur, Hamirpur, Mandi, Kangra, Shimla and Chamba

Due to small number of observations in various districts, the data were pooled to increase the number of observations to fit the production function. The results of the Cobb-Douglas production function were chosen to be described in main text because of higher value of R^2. The study of production function revealed that only the regression co-efficient in respect of fodder was turned out to be significant at 5 per cent level of significance. The value of regression co-efficient revealed that one per cent increase in fodder in all the above mentioned districts on an average will increase wool yield by 0.3914 per cent. Keeping feed, medicines, human labour and working capital constant at their geometric mean levels. The value of co-efficient of multiple determinate R^2 was computed as 0.3830 (Table 10.2) thereby, revealing that about 38 per cent of variation in wool yield is because of independent variables. The value of R^2 was found to be significant at 5 per cent level of significance.

The linear production function for Kullu, Kinnaur, Hamirpur, Mandi, Kangra, Shimla and Chamba districts pooled together is presented in Appendix III.

10.2.3 Cobb-Douglas production function for medium rabbit farmers in Kullu and Mandi districts

The Cobb-Douglas production function for medium rabbit farmers in Kullu and Mandi districts has been tried and all the variables were found to be non-significant and presented in Appendix-IV. The value of R^2 was more in case of linear production function. Therefore, in case of medium rabbit farmers the results of the linear production function were described in main text.

10.2.4 Linear production function for medium farmers in Kullu and Mandi districts of Himachal Pradesh

The results of linear production function in respect of medium farmers in Kullu and Mandi districts of Himachal Pradesh has been presented in Table 10.3. The study of the table revealed that the regression co-efficients in respect of fodder were negative and significant. One per cent increase in the quantity of

TABLE 10.2 : Cobb-douglas production function for small farmers in kullu, kinnaur, hamirpur, mandi, kangra, shimla, chamba districts of himachal pradesh

No.	Particulars	Constant	Production Elasticities				
			Feed (x_1)	Fodder (x_2)	Medicines (x_3)	Human labour (x_4)	Working capital (x_5)
1.	Production function	–1.3448	0.2985	0.3914*	0.0014	–0.0012	–0.1010
2.	Standard error	2.1968	0.1751	0.1568	0.0260	0.0706	0.0521
3.	t-value	–0.6121	1.7047	2.4962	0.0501	0.0174	1.9375
4.	R^2	0.3830					
5.	$\bar{R}^2$	0.2866					
6.	F-value	3.9733*					
7.	Degrees of freedom	32					
8.	Regression sum of square	0.7244					
9.	Error sum of square	1.1669					

Source: Primary data from the rabbit farmers.
*Significant at 5 per cent level of significance.

fodder fed to animals will reduce the wool yield by 0.0030 per cent. Keeping feed, medicines, human labour and working capital constant at their geometric mean levels. The value of co-efficient of multiple determination R^2 was computed as 0.3384 thereby revealing that 33.84 per cent of the variation in wool yield is due to the feed, fodder, medicines, human labour and working capital included in the analysis. The value of R^2 was found to be significant at 5 per cent level of significance.

10.2.5 Cobb-Douglas production function for large farmers in Kullu and Mandi districts pooled together

The linear as well as Cobb-Douglas production function for large farmers in Kullu and Mandi districts pooled together were tried. The results of the Cobb-Douglas production function has been given in Table 10.4. The study of table revealed that the regression co-efficients in favour of feed and human labour were found to be significant. One per cent increase in quantity of feed on an average will increase wool yield by 1.0614 per cent, keeping fodder, medicines, human labour and working capital constant at their geometric mean levels. The regression co-efficient of human labour were negative and significant at 5 per cent level of significance. The value of regression co-efficients of human labour revealed that one per cent further use of human labour will decrease wool yield by 0.1026 per cent keeping feed, fodder, medicine and working capital constant at their geometric mean levels. This is attributed to already over use of human labour on rabbit farms. The value of co-efficient of multiple determination R^2 was computed as 0.6455 revealing thereby that 64.55 per cent variation in the wool yield is due to the included factors in the analysis. The calculated value of F (8.7396) was greater than the table value of F (2.62), thereby, revealing that the value of R^2 was significant at one per cent levels of significance and the included variables in the analysis are significantly expressing the variation in wool yield. The data for all the districts of small, medium and large farmers were pooled to examine the position at the state level. The results in respect to linear as well as Cobb-Douglas production function for whole of the Himachal Pradesh have been presented in Appendix VI to Appendix XI. The results of the linear production function fitted to large farmers are presented in Appendix V.

TABLE 10.3 : Linear production function for medium farmers in kullu, mandi districts of Himachal Pradesh

No.	Particulars	Constant	Production Elasticities				
			Feed (x_1)	Fodder (x_2)	Medicines (x_3)	Human labour (x_4)	Working capital (x_5)
1.	Production function	62.3144	0.0012	–0.0030**	0.0026	0.0168	–0.0036
2.	Standard error	12.9684	0.0022	0.0110	0.0015	0.0168	0.0021
3.	t-value	4.8051	0.5454	2.7210	1.7333	1.0000	1.7143
4.	R^2	0.3384					
5.	$\bar{R}^2$	0.2112					
6.	F-value	2.6595*					
7.	Degrees of freedom	26					
8.	Regression sum of square	592.1783					
9.	Error sum of square	1157.87					

Source : Primary data from the rabbit farmers.
*Significant at 5 per cent level of significance.
**Significance at 1 per cent level of significance.

TABLE 10.4 : Cobb douglas production function for large farmers in kullu, mandi districts of Himachal Pradesh

No.	Particulars	Constant	*Production Elasticities*				
			Feed (x_1)	*Fodder* (x_2)	*Medicines* (x_3)	*Human labour* (x_4)	*Working capital* (x_5)
1.	Production function	–4.2795	1.0614**	–0.0697	0.0432	–0.1026*	0.0098
2.	Standard error	3.0925	0.2712	0.1835	0.0381	0.0506	0.0348
3.	t-value	–1.3838	3.9137	0.3798	1.1338	–2.0276	0.2816
4.	R^2	0.6455					
5.	$\bar{R}^2$	0.5716					
6.	F-value	8.7396**					
7.	Degrees of freedom	24					
8.	Regression sum of square	0.5840					
9.	Error sum of square	0.3207					

Source : Primary data from the rabbit farmers.
*Significant at 5 per cent level of significance.
**Significance at 1 per cent level of significance.

11

PROSPECTS OF RABBITRY FOR MEAT PRODUCTION

Rabbit meat was not popular in the hills earlier because of availability of sheep and goat meat on one hand and stigma attached to rabbit meat on the other. However, with the increase in literacy rate and health awareness among people, rabbit meat consumption has now become much easy to popularize. With the incentives provided for rabbit wool and remunerative prices for wool, wool rabbits became popular in those days. Wool rabbits was having comparative advantage over meat rabbits. Therefore, wool rabbitry became attractive and less attention was paid to meat rabbitry.

Meat rabbitry is a success story not only in advanced nations like Czechoslovakia, France, Germany, Japan, the USA and UK but in developing countries too. China at present is producing 1.20 lakh tonnes of rabbit meat and 6000 tonnes of Angora wool per year and earning hard currency of about $ 2 billion per year by export.

It is established fact the world over that when poor have access to a little more money, they spend a sizable share of it on meat to supplement their meager diet of staple grains. For all developing countries combined, per capita consumption of beef, mutton, goat, pork, rabbit meat, poultry eggs and milk rose by an average of about 50 per cent per person between 1973 and 1996. Work conducted at International Food Policy Research Institute shows that in 2020, each person in the developing world is likely to demand about 29 kilograms of meat and 63 kilograms of milk a year, up from 21 kilograms and 41 kilograms respectively in 1993. Another important contributor to rising demand for meat products is urbanization.

There are sound nutritional reasons for poor and malnourished people to wish to add more meat to their diet. "Meat contains iron, but it also helps the body to absorb iron from other foods. This trait is known as the meat factor", says Catherine Geissler of the Department of Nutrition and Dietetics at King`s College, London. A mixed omnivore diet is an easier way to get all required nutrients. Researchers showed that a fivefold increase in meat, fish and dairy consumption would lower the prevalence of anemia by 50 per cent. But with their income level, such an increase is totally infeasible, so finding ways to reduce prices of animal products is really important.

Malnutrition not only cuts short the lives and hopes of individuals, but also changes the peace and prosperity of nations. Hunger or malnutrition decreases children`s learning capacity and costs developing countries up to US $ 128 billion per year in productivity losses (FAO, estimates). In fact, the vast majority of the hungry lies in countries where agriculture is the main source of employment and income.

With rising incomes and freer markets in developing countries, it will be difficult, if not impossible, for governments to control their people's demand for meat products. The key for policy, therefore, is to ensure that meat, milk and eggs are available to the poor, who are likely to derive the greatest health benefits, and that livestock production is organized to bring the greatest benefits to the poor and to minimize damage to the environment.

The breeds of rabbit mainly used for meat purposes are Soviet Chinchilla, White Giant, Grey Giant and New Zealand White. If bred properly they achieve the expected weight of around 2.5 to 3 kg in a period of 10-15 weeks. The dressing percentage generally varies between 60-67 per cent.

Meat rabbitry is also flourishing in a few north eastern and southern states of India like Manipur, Andhra Pradesh, Tamil Nadu. In north western states such as Himachal, Jammu and Kashmir, Uttranchal, Uttar Pradesh and Punjab (Pathankot division) wool rabbitry is being taken-up. Rabbits are economical because of their early maturity (three to four months), prolificacy (7-8 young ones) and short gestation period (one month), financial investment is low with minimum risk involvement, docile and easy to handle, requires less space and simple housing, utilize vide variety of feeds and fodders, valuable skin, hairs and manure, requires less labour. The does are bred back 14 days after kindling. Kits were weaned at 28 days of age. Rabbits can turn 20 per cent of the proteins they eat into edible meat under uniform management conditions, while for chicken, pig and beef these values are 22-23, 16-18 and 8-12 per cent respectively. Rabbit meat production is more economical in terms of feed energy than other forms of meat. Rabbit meat production is therefore an attractive proposition, especially when the aim is to produce quality animal protein because they can consume cheaper fodder as a sizable part (crude fiber 15%) of their diet. A doe is introduced to the buck at four months of age. Ten days after mating, does can be palpated for pregnancy determination. Twenty-eight days after the doe is bred, the nest box is placed in the doe's cage and bedding or straw is added to the nest box. Twenty-one days after kindling, the nest box is removed, cleaned for future use. It is recommended that a doe should be culled after one year of production, which corresponds to 17 months of age.

A good doe under our type of management can give 7=8 litters. Therefore, a total yearly production = 7 litters x 8 kits = 56 kits/doe. If the mortality rate is around 15 per cent, the survival will be 56 × 0.85 = 48 kits. The local price of a kg live weight is around Rs. 50 and the average marketing weight is 2 kg at 70 days of age. This means that the total income of a doe per year is 48 rabbits × 2 kg/ rabbit × Rs. 50/kg live weight = Rs. 4,800.

Under local conditions, the doe and its offspring consume no more than 60 per cent of their total production. This means

FIG. 10 : Newzealand white-meat rabbit breed

FIG. 11 : Soviet chinchilla-meat rabbit breed

Rs. 4,800 × 0.6 = Rs. 2,880 it means net profitability is Rs. 4800-2880 = Rs. 1,920. A rabbitry unit with 10 does and a buck can generate a net profit of over Rs 19,200 a year.

Rabbit farming for meat being eco-friendly and remunerative venture for mass employment. It has an enormous potential to improve the socio-economic status of the people and health by improving quality of diet of the rural people, particularly landless, small and marginal farmers as it requires minimum capital investment, gives quick and good returns. It is a promising agri-business for eradicating hunger, alleviating poverty, helping to check migration to cities by providing opportunity of employment especially to rural youth and women.

Rabbit meat has a great relevance these days due to rich nutrition and low fat and cholesterol contents. Rabbit meat is white fine grained, delicately flavoured, nutritious, appetizing and is comparable to poultry meat. Compared with the meat of other species, rabbit meat is richer in proteins, certain vitamins and minerals, low in fat and sodium. Rabbit fat contains less stearic and oleic acids than other species and higher proportions of essential polyunsaturated fatty acids (PUFA).

Basic organoleptic properties are tenderness, juiciness and flavour. Rabbit meat does not have a strong flavour. Meat from younger rabbits is more tender *i.e.*, easy to chew. Slaughter conditions, especially the onset of rigor mortis, can modify the tenderness and juiciness of rabbit carcass. The sale of rabbit meat is largely as fresh or frozen rabbit carcass or cuts *e.g.*, loin, legs, breast, ribs, flank and forelegs. The sale of processed meat products of rabbit meat is largely limited in large super markets, hotels and limited processing channels. However, rabbit meat and meat products have tremendous potential to become popular as delicate items.

The comparative nutritive value of rabbit meat is given in Table 11.1.

TABLE 11.1 : Comparative nutritive value of rabbit meat

Type of Animal	*Protein %*	*Fat %*	*Moisture %*	*Calories per 400g (lb)*	*Cholesterol mg/kg*	*Calcium Mg/100g*	*Nicotinic acid mg/100g*	*Iron mg/100g*	*Phosphorous mg/100g*	*Vitamin B_6 mg/100g*	*Sodium mg/100g*
Rabbit	20.8	10.2	27.9	795	50	20	13.0	1.5	356	0.45	40
Chicken	20.0	11.2	67.0	810	60	10	8.0	1.5	240	0.45	70
Veal	18.8	14.0	66.0	910	100	12	5.0	3.0	195	1.5	65
Lamb	15.7	27.7	55.0	1420	100	10	5.0	1.5	165	0.3	75
Pork	11.9	45.0	42.0	2050	105	10	4.5	2.5	195	0.3	70

12
SUMMARY AND CONCLUSIONS

12.1 Introduction

Rabbits give high income because of their early maturity, ecofriendly, prolificacy (7-8 young ones) and short gestation period (one months). The per year collection of wool from a rabbit is 800-1000 g and average meat comes to be 4 kg which is three times higher than a yield from sheep. The origin of Angora rabbit is believed to be Abkara (Turkey) and Asia Minor. At present the total wool production at world level is about 13,000 tonne per year. The focus of the developed countries at present is on rabbitry for meat production. At present the leading rabbit meat producing countries are former Soviet Union, China, France, Italy, Spain, USA, Mexico, Cuba, Brazil, Japan, Ghana, Egypt, Algeria and Sudan. Angora rabbits for the first time were introduced in 1962 in Kullu district of Himachal Pradesh. Himachal Pradesh has emerged as a major Angora wool producing state in country. The economic viability alongwith existing status of rabbit industry and problems and prospects of this industry needs to be investigated. Therefore, the present investigation was undertaken with the following specific objectives:

12.2 Objectives of the Study

The specific objectives of the study were:

1. To study the trend in rabbit wool production in Himachal Pradesh.
2. To study the cost and profitability of wool production and to work out the optimum size alongwith break even point of rabbitry farms in Himachal Pradesh.

3. To study the market structure of rabbit wool in Himachal Pradesh.
4. To study the technological gap between existing and potential levels of rabbit wool in Himachal Pradesh.
5. To highlight the problems and constraints of rabbit wool enterprises and suggest suitable measures to overcome them.

12.3 Methodology

The present study covers the whole of the state of Himachal Pradesh. The state has been divided into four agro-climatic zones and wool rabbitry can be taken-up in the three agro climatic zone of Himachal Pradesh. The complete enumeration of rabbit farms was done and farms were categorised into three categories with the help of cube root frequency method viz., small farms with less than 25 rabbits, medium farms with 25-150 rabbits and large farms with more than 150 rabbits. The study is based on primary as well as secondary data. The data were analysed by employing linear and exponential production functions, students t-test, F-test, Chi-square test and Cobb-Douglas production function apart from other simple mathematical tests.

The Main Findings of the Study are

12.4 Socio-economic and Structural Parameters

Rabbitry as a profession in Himachal Pradesh is not older than two decades and majority of the rabbit entrepreneurs are in the age group of 30-60 years. Majority of the rabbit entrepreneurs are literate about 13 per cent of them are degree holders. Rabbitry has been adopted as a subsidiary occupation by about 73 per cent of rabbit entrepreneurs. However, agriculture is the main profession on all the categories of farms and 51 per cent of rabbit entrepreneurs had taken-up agriculture as primary profession. The land holding size of rabbit entrepreneurs ranged between 0.47 to 0.52 ha with average size of 0.47 ha at all farm situation. About 80 per cent of the rabbit entrepreneurs got a formal training and majority of them acquired training for a period of a week. According to rabbit entrepreneurs training for a period of a week is sufficient to sum a rabbitry unit.

Capital investment per hundred rabbits on different size of farms revealed negative relationship between size of farms and investment. The investment was computed as Rs. 2,34,780, Rs. 46,437, Rs. 29,754 and Rs. 41,059 on small, medium, large and all farms respectively. The major share of capital investment was devoted to rabbit sheds and accounted for 59.62 per cent of total capital investment.

The average gross income from all sources on small, medium, large and all farms situation was Rs. 6,504, Rs. 7,444, Rs 19,217 and Rs. 9,798 on small, medium, large and all farms situation respectively. On small farms the maximum income was earned from cultivation of vegetable crops (40.49%). On medium farms rabbitry was the highest contributor (34.71%) on all large farms too, rabbitry was the top most contributor (65.28%). On all farms situation the rabbitry accounted for 40.22 per cent of gross income followed by vegetable cultivation (14.35%).

The per rabbit per day feed consumption and size of farms were negatively correlated. The per day per rabbit feed consumption was 140, 130 and 120 grams respectively on small, medium and large farms respectively. The value of feed fed per rabbit per day was estimated to be Rs. 0.95, Rs. 1.28, Rs. 0.76 and Rs. 0.89 on small, medium, large and all farms respectively.

The study of gender employment revealed that about 79 per cent of entrepreneurs were men and 21 per cent were women.

Existing rabbitry units in Himachal Pradesh are less than two decades old and started coming-up in 1984. The maximum number of units were established in 1996. At present the maximum number of rabbitry units were recorded in Mandi district followed by Kullu district in Himachal Pradesh.

In Solan district maximum number of rabbit farms had been closed as majority of them were small farms and had acquired rabbits free of cost from Government agencies. Over a period of three years there has been no closure of rabbit farms in Mandi and Hamirpur districts of Himachal Pradesh. The next minimum closure was in Kullu district (15.38%) of Himachal Pradesh. The maximum change in number of rabbit farms was observed in Solan district of Himachal Pradesh where the number of rabbit farms decreased from 55 to 12 and showed a change of 78.18 per cent. The total number of rabbit farms has decreased from 170 to 96 and showing a decline of 43.52 per cent. However, total number of rabbits in the state has increased from 14,300 rabbits in 1997-98 to 15, 699 rabbits in 1999-2000 and showing an increase of 9.57 per cent. This is attributed to closing down of small uneconomical farms and increase in number of rabbits of large farms, which are running in profit.

12.5 Wool Production

The total rabbit wool production in Himachal Pradesh was estimated at 7127 kilograms per year. The study of growth rates in total wool production (including sheep wool) revealed non-significant linear (0.893%) as well as exponential growth rates (0.903%). The co-efficient of variation in total wool production in Himachal Pradesh was computed as 10.87 per cent. The quantity of rabbit wool procured by Himachal Pradesh State Wool Federation showed a non-significant linear (4.528%) and well as compound growth rate (3.104%) from 1989-90 to 2001-2002. The co-efficient of variation was computed as 110 per cent showing very high fluctuations in the quantity of rabbit wool purchased by Wool Federation over the years. The price paid by Himachal Pradesh State Wool Federation over the years showed a declining trend from 1997-98 onwards. The co-efficient of variation for the average price was computed as 21.62 per cent.

The linear and compound growth rates were turned out to be non-significant at 5 per cent level of significance.

During the last decade customs tariff duty had been lowered from 60 per cent to 15 per cent by Government of India, which has increased the access of international exporter and prices in domestic market are falling. In 1993-94 when customs tariff was increased from 60 to 85 per cent, the prices increased from Rs. 526 to Rs. 696. In India fine wool is imported from Australia, Canada, China, France, Korea, New Zealand, USA and Switzerland.

12.6 Infrastructure Facilities

The study of infrastructural facilities revealed that except railway station other basic facilities exists within a radius of 5 kilometre to majority of the rabbit entrepreneurs.

The total cost of rearing a unit of 100 rabbits came out to be Rs. 1,24,968, Rs. 69,232, Rs. 51,536 and Rs. 58,330 on small, medium, large and all farms situation, respectively. On small farms the total cost constituted 36 per cent and variable cost 64 per cent of total cost. The interest on fixed capital and cost of feed were the major components in fixed and variable costs respectively. On medium farms fixed and variable costs accounted for about 20 and 80 per cent of total cost respectively. Similar pattern was observed on large farms too. On all farms depreciation on animals and interest on fixed capital were the major items in fixed cost and cost of feed and labour charges were the main components of variable cost.

The installation of feed manufacturing plant from locally available feed resources at Mandi (H.P.) had reduced the cost of feed to Rs. 650 per quintal as compared to Rs. 850 per quintal of feed manufactured by multinational companies. This is likely to reduce the cost of production significantly. The study of benefit-cost ratio revealed that wool was the major source of income accounting for about 76 per cent of the gross returns.

The study of gross returns in the present scenario of recession in rabbit wool industry revealed that small and medium farms were running in loss, however, large farms were meeting out their cost of production. Benefit-cost ratio was observed to be 0.40, 0.73, 1.0 and 0.72 on small, medium, large and all farm situations respectively. The per kilogram cost of wool production decreased with the increase in farm size. It was highest on small farms (Rs. 2648), followed by medium farms (Rs. 1323) and Rs. 941 on large farms. On all farms the total cost of wool production was computed as Rs. 1364 per kilogram of wool production. The net returns per kilogram of wool production were negative on small and medium farms. However, they were marginally positive on large farms. At the existing level of returns the rabbit farms cannot remain in production in the long run. The large farms are making a profit of Rs. 201 per kilogram of wool over variable cost. The net returns over total cost of a kilogram of wool production were just Rs. 3 per kilogram of wool.

The break-even size of small farms was worked out to be 29 against the existing size of 8 rabbits. For medium rabbit entrepreneurs the break even size of herd was 148 against existing size of 83 only. The break-even herd size for large farms was 332 against existing of 261. However, on all farms situation the break-even herd size was worked out to be 166 against the existing size of 90 rabbits. The extent of deviation between existing and break-even size of herd on different size of farms revealed that extent of deviation decreased with the increase in farm size. The maximum extent of deviation was observed on small farms (72.41%) followed by medium farms (43.92%) and large farms (21.38%). The extent of deviation in the size of herd between existing and break-even size was worked out to be 45.78 per cent on all farm situation.

12.7 Marketing Channels and Marketing Costs

Looking at the problems of rabbit entrepreneurs the Government of Himachal Pradesh established Himachal Pradesh State Cooperative Wool Procurement and Marketing Federation (WPMF) in 1988-89. Earlier recession in the rabbit industry was in 1989 when prices of rabbit wool were slashed from Rs. 1400 per kilograms in mid 80's to Rs. 450 per kg and as a consequence 90 per cent of Angora units were wiped out in the state during 1989. Since January 1988 the declining graph of prices has again become a matter of grave concern to the farmers. The price of wool was slashed from Rs. 1000 per kilogram to Rs. 750 per kg of "A" grade Angora wool.

Rabbit wool had a great marketing potential, as there is no animal fibre, which had the same lightness, softness and purity of fleece as Angora. The typical, weight of Angora wool would be 1.1 g per cm^3, whereas the next lightness wool of Merino would weigh approximately 1.3 g per cm^3. In textile terminology, the tex number of Angora wool is 7, meaning thereby that it is possible to spin 1000 meters of yarn from 7 gram of Angora wool. Whereas, the tex number for sheep`s wool is 20.

The study of prevailing market prices from 1980 to 2001 showed that prices varied between Rs. 300 to Rs. 1000 a kilogram. There has been a phenomenal rise in prices during the years from 1994 to 1997. However, the peak price of Rs. 1000 could not be attained later on. This fluctuation resulted in fluctuation of flock size. The study of marketing channels revealed that majority of the rabbit entrepreneurs marketed the wool through Himachal Pradesh State Wool Federation. The other conspicuous channels were through traders and large producers which also acted as traders in collection of rabbit wool. The study of the marketing costs revealed that the transportation charges in all districts formed the major component of costs. The next highest charges were on shearing of rabbit wool.

12.8 Technological Gap

The study of technological gap revealed that maximum technological gap of 17.80 per cent existed in case of feed followed by size of cages (16.78%) and light (15.62%).

The negative value in technological gap showed the over use of inputs and maximum negative technological gap existed in case of medication (-171.8%) followed by roughages (–89.91%) and labour (-69.47%). The over use of the inputs is due to small size of farms.

12.9 Problems and Constraints

The problems faced by rabbit entrepreneurs have been classified as production, financial, marketing and institutional problems. The gravity of the problem and farm size had an inverse relationship. The gravity of problems decreased with the increase in farm size. The problem of non-availability of feed at appropriate time was reported by about 52 per cent of rabbit entrepreneurs.

About 72 per cent of rabbit farms on all farms situation revealed the problem of high prices of feed. Scarcity of fodder was reported by about 12 per cent of the rabbit entrepreneurs. The problem of non-availability of cages, feeders and waterers was reported by about 18 per cent of rabbit entrepreneurs.

About 22 per cent of rabbit entrepreneurs reported the problem of veterinary aid when required. The non-availability of labour was experienced by about 41 per cent of rabbit entrepreneurs on all farms category. The problem of fresh blood to check inbreeding was reported by about 32 per cent of entrepreneurs on all farms category. Eighty six per cent of the entrepreneurs were not maintaining farm records. The study of financial problems revealed that non-availability of credit at appropriate time was reported by 92.31 per cent of rabbit entrepreneurs on all farms. However, 92 per cent of rabbit entrepreneurs on all farms reported that credit was inadequate.

The loan limit is Rs. 2430 for a unit of 10 females + 2 males for furl meat and Rs. 8850 for a unit of wool type breeding rabbits. However, large entrepreneurs can take loan for more than one unit. Banks assume that daily requirements of about two hours per unit for adult rabbits and the progeny, scheme would provide additional employment of 90 days per year per unit. However, majority of the farmers were not aware of loan facility.

Among marketing problems the unremunerative prices of wool and meat were reported by hundred per cent of the farms. The high prices of breeder rabbits was revealed by 88 per cent of rabbit entrepreneurs. The seasonal demand of wool products was revealed by about 99 per cent of rabbit entrepreneurs on all farm situation.

About 54 per cent of rabbit entrepreneurs on all farms situation revealed that the government should fix support price for rabbit wool. Eighty eight per cent of the farmers were of the view that the adult rabbits are not being sold at remunerative prices either for breeding purpose or establishing the new units by other farmers. About 99 per cent of rabbit entrepreneurs revealed that the demand for rabbit wool and other products is seasonal. Among institutional problems lack of extension facilities was reported by maximum number of rabbit entrepreneurs (84.62%). The non-availability of package of practices was revealed by about 83 per cent of rabbit entrepreneurs on all farms situation.

12.10 Regression Analysis

The regression analysis on small farms in Solan district and Kullu, Kinnaur, Hamirpur, Mandi, Kangra, Shimla, Chamba (pooled together) revealed that yield of wool could be increased if more fodder is fed to animals. The regression co-efficient of medicines was with negative sign in Solan district and significant and showed that further use of medicines will reduce wool yield. The value of R^2 was found to be significant at 5 per cent level of significance. However, on medium farms in Kullu and Mandi districts (pooled together) the value of the regression co-efficient for fodder was negative. However, on large farms the wool yield could be increased if rabbits are fed more quantity of feed and 1 per cent increase in feed will increase the yield by 1.0614 per cent keeping fodder, medicines, working capital and human labour constant at their geometric mean levels.

12.11 Meat Production

Meat rabbitry like other countries has a future in our country too. A rabbitry unit of 10 does and a buck can generate a net profit of over Rs. 19,200 a year. Meat rabbitry being ecofriendly and remunerative venture suits for small and marginal farmers as it requires minimum capital investment, gives quick and good returns. Rabbit meat has a great relevance these days due to rich nutrition and low fat and cholesterol contents. Compared with the meat of other species rabbit meat is richer in proteins, certain vitamins and minerals, low in F at and sodium.

12.12 Policy Implications

- For making rabbit as a viable livestock species it has to be introduced on scientific lines. The Government of India and Indian Council of Agricultural Research may open a National Centre for Rabbit Research and Training as has been done in case of sheep, goat, horses, camels, buffaloes and poultry thereby accepting rabbit as also one of the important livestock species having overall multifacet utility to the country. Training of scientists, technicians and farmers should also be a component objective of such a National Research Centre.

- Case of slashing down the import duty abruptly from 60 per cent to 15 per cent should be taken-up with the Ministry of Commerce, Government of India so that the prices of the imported wool are at par with the domestic produce and domestic production is encouraged.

- The rabbit entrepreneurs should form the Co-operatives and should shear the wool at same time after same interval so that the handloom industry gets a raw material of uniform size and quality for manufacturing products. This will increase the demand of rabbit wool by product manufacturing industry.

- For sound and sure market for Angora wool produced by rabbit entrepreneurs, some organized marketing agencies in private and public sectors should come forward for readily purchase of Angora wool on adequate support price so that the Angora farmers are sure about the timely and proper sale of this costly commodity. National Wool Board, Hosiery Industry, Handicraft Board and Khadi Gramogyog etc., may also come forward to utilize this luxury animal fibre for home and abroad markets, thus, avoiding exploitation of small farmers from middlemen and vested interests.

- There is a demand of good Angora rabbits by some government agencies and other commercial concerns within the state as well as in other states. If the sale or disposal of surplus animals is organized through some state/private marketing agencies can also bring economic gains to Angora farmers.

- A success story of manufacturing rabbit feed from locally available resources in Mandi district of Himachal Pradesh has reduced the price of feed from Rs. 850 for commercial brand feed to Rs. 650 per quintal. This may be replicated in other districts too.

- In commercial rabbit production, high cost of labour can be reduced through automation of commercial rabbitries with respect to feeding, watering, cleaning systems as well as shearing techniques.

- For providing adequate health coverage to Angora rabbits, the veterinary departments of respective states/universities/research organisations should ensure providing proper and timely prophylactic and curative means besides giving necessary advisement to farmers in these respects. Mobile veterinary vans and printed literature regarding control of some important Angora rabbit diseases will help to a great extent in alleviating the disease problems.

- To overcome most of the constraints and field problems of successful Angora rabbit entrepreneurs. The integrated team comprising of Animal breeder, health specialist, economist, nutritionist and animal husbandry expert should visit the farms located in far off areas of the state.

- The problem of inbreeding can be checked by providing fresh blood of scientific tested progeny. This work should be undertaken by government agency at affordable rates.

- The provision of training to rabbit entrepreneurs should be strengthened and package of practices should be made readily available. Involvement and training of farm women has to be further encouraged. Awareness among the entrepreneurs will abridge the gap between existing and recommended levels of inputs.

- Rabbitry for meat should also be popularized. As meat of rabbit is low in cholesterol and fats and rich in minerals and vitamins. In cold regions the rabbit meat can easily be popularized and it will have good market in the villages itself.

- Small demonstration units of rabbit rearing may be initiated and attached to certain schools or vocational training institutes. These units should be managed by the student groups under the expert guidance of an extension worker, on the pattern of "Earn While You Learn" scheme.

- Rabbit units established by obtaining rabbits as free of cost has led to maximum closure. Therefore, the scheme of distribution of rabbits, free of cost should be discouraged so that only real interested entrepreneurs take-up the profession by investing money on it and flourish the business.

APPENDIX-I

RABBIT WOOL PRODUCTION AND QUALITY IN DIFFERENT BREEDS OF ANGORA RABBITS

Breed/strain	*Annual Wool Prod. (g)*	*Fibre Length diameter (cm) (microns)*	*Fibre Hair (%)*	*Guard*
Russian Angora	250–300	6–8	14–18	12–18
British Angora	400–500	6–7	12–14	
German Angora	700–800	6–8	10–12	4–6
Crossbred Angora (Russia x British x German)	400–500	5–7	12–14	5–7
Danish Angora	800–1000	7–9	12–18	10–15

APPENDIX-II

LINEAR PRODUCTION FUNCTION FOR SMALL FARMERS IN DISTRICT SOLAN OF HIMACHAL PRADESH

No.	Particulars	Constant	Production Elasticities				
			Feed (x_1)	*Fodder* (x_2)	*Medicines* (x_3)	*Human labour* (x_4)	*Working capital* (x_5)
1.	Production function	4.7529	–0.0025	0.0059*	–0.0015	0.0044	0.0007
2.	Standard error	22.7872	0.0021	0.0021	0.0006	0.0052	0.0012
3.	t-value	0.2086	–1.1931	2.7575	2.5536	0.8376	0.6185
4.	R^2	0.2583					
5.	$\bar{R}^2$	0.1794					
6.	F-value	3.2734*					
7.	Degrees of freedom	47					
8.	Regression sum of square	2350.838					
9.	Error sum of square	6750.679					

Source : Primary data from the rabbit farmers.
*Significant at 5 per cent level of significance.

APPENDIX-III

LINEAR PRODUCTION FUNCTION FOR SMALL FARMERS IN KULLU, KINNAUR, HAMIRPUR, MANDI, KANGRA, SHIMLA, CHAMBA DISTRICTS OF HIMACHAL PRADESH

No.	*Particulars*	*Constant*	*Production Elasticities*				
			Feed (x_1)	*Fodder* (x_2)	*Medicines* (x_3)	*Human labour* (x_4)	*Working capital* (x_5)
1.	Production function	15.4685	0.0036*	0.0024	–0.0002	0.0015	–0.0007
2.	Standard error	11.3961	0.0015	0.0010	0.0002	0.0054	0.0006
3.	t-value	1.3573	2.4000	2.4000	–1.0000	0.2777	1.1667
4.	R^2	0.2710					
5.	$\bar{R}^2$	0.1571					
6.	F-value	2.3792					
7.	Degrees of freedom	32					
8.	Regression sum of square	1239.0580					
9.	Error sum of square	3333.0390					

Source : Primary data from the rabbit farmers.
*Significant at 5 per cent level of significance.

APPENDIX-IV

COBB-DOUGLAS PRODUCTION FUNCTION FOR MEDIUM FARMERS IN KULLU AND MANDI DISTRICT OF HIMACHAL PRADESH

No.	Particulars	Constant	*Production Elasticities*				
			Feed (x_1)	Fodder (x_2)	Medicines (x_3)	Human labour (x_4)	Working capital (x_5)
1.	Production function	4.6251	0.1721	–0.2827	0.0674	0.0454	–0.0619
2.	Standard error	2.2149	0.2202	0.1556	0.0469	0.1307	0.1304
3.	t-value	2.0882	0.7815	–1.8470	1.4371	0.3474	–0.4747
4.	R^2	0.2176					
5.	$\bar{R}^2$	0.0671					
6.	F-value	1.4463					
7.	Degrees of freedom	26					
8.	Regression sum of square	0.1505					
9.	Error sum of square	0.5410					

Source : Primary data from the rabbit farmers.

APPENDIX-V

LINEAR PRODUCTION FUNCTION FOR LARGE FARMERS IN KULLU AND MANDI DISTRICTS OF HIMACHAL PRADESH

No.	Particulars	Constant	Production Elasticities				
			Feed (x_1)	Fodder (x_2)	Medicines (x_3)	Human labour (x_4)	Working capital (x_5)
1.	Production function	12.7015	0.0119**	–0.0013	0.0016	–0.0953*	–0.0009
2.	Standard error	18.0718	0.0031	0.0013	0.0014	0.0401	0.0033
3.	t-value	0.7028	3.8387	1.0000	1.1428	2.3765	0.2727
4.	R^2	0.6662					
5.	$\bar{R}^2$	0.5967					
6.	F-value	9.5812**					
7.	Degrees of freedom	24					
8.	Regression sum of square	1443.7990					
9.	Error sum of square	723.3131					

Source : Primary data from the rabbit farmers.
*Significant at 5 per cent level of significance.
**Significant at 1 per cent level of significance.

APPENDIX-VI

LINEAR PRODUCTION FUNCTION FOR SMALL FARMERS FOR WHOLE OF HIMACHAL PRADESH

No.	Particulars	Constant	*Production Elasticities*				
			Feed (x_1)	*Fodder* (x_2)	*Medicines* (x_3)	*Human labour* (x_4)	*Working capital* (x_5)
1.	Production function	43.0985	0.0024	0.0001	-0.0001	–0.0003	–0.0010
2.	Standard error	8.1622	0.0015	0.0002	0.0003	0.0011	0.0007
3.	t-value	5.2802	1.6	0.5000	0.3333	–0.2727	1.4286
4.	$\underline{R}^2$	0.0745					
5.	R^2	0.0219					
6.	F-value	1.4178					
7.	Degrees of freedom	88					
8.	Regression sum of square	1413,929					
9.	Error sum of square	17551.87					

Source : Primary data from the rabbit farmers.
*Significant at 5 per cent level of significance.
**Significant at 1 per cent level of significance.

APPENDIX-VII

COBB-DOUGLAS PRODUCTION FUNCTION FOR SMALL FARMERS FOR WHOLE OF HIMACHAL PRADESH

No.	*Particulars*	*Constant*	*Production Elasticities*				
			Feed (x_1)	*Fodder* (x_2)	*Medicines* (x_3)	*Human labour* (x_4)	*Working capital* (x_5)
1.	Production function	–0.0102	0.3114*	0.2144*	–0.0787	0.0945	–0.1418
2.	Standard error	1.6180	0.1511	0.0993	0.0278	0.0504	0.0603
3.	t-value	0.0630	2.0608	2.1591	2.8309	0.5333	–2.3516
4.	$\underline{R}^2$	0.1671					
5.	R^2	0.1198					
6.	F-value	3.5299**					
7.	Degrees of freedom	88					
8.	Regression sum of square	1.3769					
9.	Error sum of square	6.8651					

Source : Primary data from the rabbit farmers.
*Significant at 5 per cent level of significance.
**Significant at 1 per cent level of significance.

APPENDIX-VIII

LINEAR PRODUCTION FUNCTION FOR MEDIUM FARMERS FOR WHOLE OF HIMACHAL PRADESH

No.	Particulars	Constant	*Production Elasticities*				
			Feed (x_1)	Fodder (x_2)	Medicines (x_3)	Human labour (x_4)	Working capital (x_5)
1.	Production function	29.9356	0.0043*	–0.0003	0.0023	0.0167	0.0003
2.	Standard error	9.7149	0.0020	0.0010	0.0016	0.0188	0.0022
3.	t-value	3.0814	2.1500	–0.3000	1.4375	0.8882	0.1360
4.	$\underline{R}^2$	0.2465					
5.	R^2	0.1499					
6.	F-value	2.5512					
7.	Degrees of freedom	39					
8.	Regression sum of square	886.9306					
9.	Error sum of square	2711.727					

Source : Primary data from the rabbit farmers.
*Significant at 5 per cent level of significance.
**Significant at 1 per cent level of significance.

APPENDIX-IX

COBB-DOUGLAS PRODUCTION FUNCTION FOR MEDIUM FARMERS FOR WHOLE OF HIMACHAL PRADESH

No.	Particulars	Constant	Production Elasticities				
			Feed (x_1)	Fodder (x_2)	Medicines (x_3)	Human labour (x_4)	Working capital (x_5)
1.	Production function	0.5834	0.3668*	–0.0533	0.0872*	0.0273	0.0019
2.	Standard error	1.5058	0.1733	0.1340	0.0430	0.0793	0.0417
3.	t-value	0.3874	2.1165	0.3977	2.0279	0.3442	0.0455
4.	R^2	0.2555					
5.	$\bar{R}^2$	0.1600					
6.	F-value	2.6772					
7.	Degrees of freedom	39					
8.	Regression sum of square	0.3285					
9.	Error sum of square	0.9572					

Source : Primary data from the rabbit farmers.
*Significant at 5 per cent level of significance.
**Significant at 1 per cent level of significance.

APPENDIX-X

LINEAR PRODUCTION FUNCTION FOR LARGE FARMERS FOR WHOLE OF HIMACHAL PRADESH

No.	Particulars	Constant	*Production Elasticities*				
			Feed (x_1)	Fodder (x_2)	Medicines (x_3)	Human labour (x_4)	Working capital (x_5)
1.	Production function	76.3492	-0.0036	-0.0013	0.0035	-0.0774	-0.0050
2.	Standard error	22.8431	0.0027	0.0020	0.0021	0.0623	0.0051
3.	t-value	3.3423	-1.3330	-0.6500	1.6666	-1.2423	-0.9803
4.	$\underline{R}^2$	0.2515					
5.	R^2	0.1018					
6.	F-value	1.6801					
7.	Degrees of freedom	25					
8.	Regression sum of square	612.7369					
9.	Error sum of square	1823.45					

Source : Primary data from the rabbit farmers.
*Significant at 5 per cent level of significance.
**Significant at 1 per cent level of significance.

APPENDIX-XI

COBB DOUGLAS PRODUCTION FUNCTION FOR LARGE FARMERS FOR WHOLE OF HIMACHAL PRADESH

No.	Particulars	Constant	Production Elasticities				
			Feed (x_1)	Fodder (x_2)	Medicines (x_3)	Human labour (x_4)	Working capital (x_5)
1.	Production function	6.9253	–0.1616*	–0.2124	0.0926	–0.0672	–0.0317
2.	Standard error	2.5737	0.0760	0.2433	0.0492	0.0673	0.0452
3.	t-value	2.6907	–2.1263	–0.8729	1.8821	–0.9985	–0.7013
4.	$\underline{R}^2$	0.3916					
5.	R^2	0.2699					
6.	F-value	3.2186*					
7.	Degrees of freedom	25					
8.	Regression sum of square	0.3894					
9.	Error sum of square	0.6049					

Source : Primary data from the rabbit farmers.
*Significant at 5 per cent level of significance.
**Significant at 1 per cent level of significance.

BIBLIOGRAPHY

Ashok Kumar, "Impact of Risk and Uncertainty on Vegetable Production and Farm Income in Kangra District of Himachal Pradesh". Ph.D thesis (unpublished) Himachal Pradesh Krishi Vishvavidyalaya, Palampur, 1988.

Bhat, T.K. (1999). "Angora Rabbit Farming in the Hilly Regions of India". *Himachal Veterinary Journal*. 3: 61–63.

Cheeke, P.R., Patton, N.M., and Templeton G.S.(1982). *Rabbit Production*. (5th edition), Interstate Printers and Publishers, Inc, USA.

Guleria, J.S.(2001). "Characteristics of Successful Entrepreneurs in Rabbit Farming". Technical Lectures on Rabbit Production for Subject Matter Workshop-cum-Seminar on Rabbit Farming. Sponsored by Directorate of Extension, Ministry of Agriculture, Government of India. Organized by Directorate of Extension Education through Department of Animal Nutrition, College of Veterinary and Animal Sciences, CSK Himachal Pradesh Krishi Vishvavidyalaya, Palampur -176 062. September 6–13, 2001: 17–18.

Gulyani, R. and Singh, D.(1990). "Useful Tips for Increasing Angora Wool Production", *Indian Farmers Digest*, 23 (5) : 25–2 7.

James, I. and MC. Nitt (1986). "Waste Water in Rabbitries", *The Journal of Applied Rabbit Research*, 9 (2).

Jithendran, K.P. (1998). "Rabbit Production in Sub-Himalayan Region". *Indian Farming*. May 1998: 15–19.

Katoch, B.S.(2001). "Prospects of Rabbit Production in India". Technical Lectures on Rabbit Production for Subject Matter Workshop-cum-Seminar on Rabbit Farming. Sponsored by

Directorate of Extension, Ministry of Agriculture, Government of India. Organized by Directorate of Extension Education through Department of Animal Nutrition, College of Veterinary and Animal Sciences, CSK Himachal Pradesh Krishi Vishvavidyalaya, Palampur -176 062. September 6-13, 2001:1-4.

Katoch, B.S. (2001). "Economical Feeding of Commercial Rabbits". Technical Lectures on Rabbit Production for Subject Matter Workshop-cum-Seminar on Rabbit Farming. Sponsored by Directorate of Extension, Ministry of Agriculture, Government of India. Organized by Directorate of Extension Education through Department of Animal Nutrition, College of Veterinary and Animal Sciences, CSK Himachal Pradesh Krishi Vishvavidyalaya, Palampur -176 062. September 6–13, 2001: 60–66.

Katoch, Sanjeet (2001). "Breeds and Breeding of Rabbits". Technical Lectures on Rabbit Production for Subject Matter Workshop-cum-Seminar on Rabbit Farming. Sponsored by Directorate of Extension, Ministry of Agriculture, Government of India. Organized by Directorate of Extension Education through Department of Animal Nutrition, College of Veterinary and Animal Sciences, CSK Himachal Pradesh Krishi Vishvavidyalaya, Palampur-176 062. September 6–13, 2001: 19–21.

Kishore Kamal and Krishma Shamshi (2001). "Angora Rabbit–A Boon to Farmers and Woollen Industry". Technical Lectures on Rabbit Production for Subject Matter Workshop-cum-Seminar on Rabbit Farming. Sponsored by Directorate of Extension, Ministry of Agriculture, Government of India. Organized by Directorate of Extension Education through Department of Animal Nutrition, College of Veterinary and Animal Sciences, CSK Himachal Pradesh Krishi Vishvavidyalaya, Palampur-176 062. September 6–13, 2001 : 5-9.

Kumar, B. M. Arif, D.S. Khati and M.C. Joshi (1992). "Angora Rabbit keeping for wool production". *Farmers and Parliament*, 27 (10) : 5-6.

Lall, D., Vaid, J. and Negi, S.S.(1984). "Angora Rabbits for Higher Wool Production", *Farmers Journal*, July: 50–52.

Lebas, F., Coudert, P., Rouvier, R. and Rochambeau, H.(1986). *The Rabbit, Husbandry Health and Production*, FAO Publication, Rome.

Lemaire, N. and Tasset P. (1987). "Diagnostic d'une foliere en mutation", 1 Angora francais en 1987. Memoire de fin d'etudes del Ecole Superieure d Agriculture d,Angers, : 149. (down loaded from internet).

Martineze, G.M. (1987). "Technical and Economic results of Rabbit Production", *WAERSA*, 2125, 31 (4).

Makhohlane, B.J.T. (1987). "Rabbit as a Production Animal", *WAERSA* 1563, 31 (3).

Manuja, N.K. (1990). "Rabbit Housing", Paper presented at *National Seminar on Angora Rabbit Farming* held at CSIR Complex, Palampur.

Ossard, H, R.G. The Bault, J.L. Vrillon, D. Allain and H. De Rochambeau (1995). "Economic overview of the French and World markets for Angora rabbit wool". *European Fine Fibre Network*. Occasional Publication No. 5 (1995): 35–46.

Phull, R.K. and Phull, A. (1989). *Khargosh Palan*, Kittem Kittoo Angora Rabbit Farm Publication, Palampur.

Phull, Archana (1991). "Economic Analysis of Rabbit Fanning in Kangra District of Himachal Pradesh". M.Sc. Thesis (Unpublished), Himachal Pradesh Krishi Vishvavidyalaya, Palampur.

Phull, R.K.(1990). "Angora Rabbit Farming in Kangra Valley – Problems and Suggestions", Paper Presented at *National Seminar on Angora Rabbit Farming* held at CSIR Complex, Palampur.

Rao, B.D., Reddy T.G. and Singh, C.B. (1991). "Economics of Buffalo Milk Production on Commercial Dairy Farms". *Indian Journal of Dairy Science* 44(1): 15–19.

Rai, R.B., Singh, R.N. and Rajendra Prashad (1987). "Opening a Rabbitry", *Indian Farmers Digest*, Vol. 20, No. 6: 7-9.

Rougeot, J. and Thebault R-G. (1984): Le lapin Angora, sa toison, son elevage. Le Point Veterinaire, Ed. Maisons Alfort, France,: 182. (down loaded from internet).

Sawal, R.K., DR. Bhatia and V. Bhasin (1991). "Feed-related toxic factor in rabbit farming *Indian Farming* Vol. 45, No. 9, Dec.: 28–30.

Saxena, B.C., Bhagwan Dass and Devendra Kumar (1998). "Rabbit Fanning – A Profitable Enterprise". *Indian Farming*, July: 24–25 and 32.

Schlolaut, W. (1980). The Angora rabbit Deutsche G.T.Z., Gmbh Ed. : 98 (down loaded from internet).

Scholaut, W., Gekle, L., Lange, K., Paufier, S. and Zimmerman (1985). E., *A Compendium of Rabbit Production*, Published by Deutsche Gesellschaft fur Techaische Zusaminenerbeit (GTZ) Gmbtt, Pay Hammers Kjp,d Weg 1+2, D 6236 Eschborn 1 Federal Republic of Germany.

Schlolaut, W. (1980). The Angora rabbit Deutsche G.T.Z., Gmbh Ed., p 98 (down loaded from internet).

Sharma, A.K., Prakash Mehta and S.K. Sharma (1998). "Economic viability, Technological Gap Problems and Future Strategy to Enhance Export of Rabbit Wool in Himachal Pradesh". *Seminar on Management of Export Marketing of High Value Farm Strategies*, Hissar :152–160.

Sharma, A.K. (1998). "Untapped Potential of Rabbitry". *The Tribune* December 5, 1998.

Sharma, A.K. (2000). "Rabbitry — A Hidden Treasure — Needs Attention". *The Himachal Reporter*, July 31, 2000.

Sharma, Alok. (2001). "Popularization of Rabbit Farming Amongst Farmers — Concepts and Constraints". Technical Lectures on Rabbit Production for Subject Matter Workshop-cum-Seminar on Rabbit Farming. Sponsored by Directorate of Extension,

Ministry of Agriculture, Government of India. Organized by Directorate of Extension Education through Department of Animal Nutrition, College of Veterinary and Animal Sciences, CSK Himachal Pradesh Krishi Vishvavidyalaya, Palampur-176 062. September 6–13, 2001: 10–16.

Singh, B. (1990). "Angora Rabbit Nutrition", Paper presented at National Seminar on Angora Rabbit Farming held at CSIR Complex, Palampur.

Singh, N.P. (1996). "Nutrition and Feeding of Rabbits for Meat". *Indian Farming,* 46 (4) July: 30–35.

Singh, R.N., Rai, R.B. and Rajendra Prashad (1987). "Care of Rabbits", *Indian Farmers Digest,* 20 (6) : 21–25.

Sood, Pankaj (2001). "Reproduction in Rabbits". Technical lectures on rabbit production for subject matter workshop-cum-seminar on rabbit fanning Department of Animal Nutrition, College of Veterinary and Animal Sciences, CSK Himachal Pradesh Krishi Vishvavidyalaya, Palampur - 176 062: 129–31.

Sudheer, S.N. Kumarvchi and Ajit Chakrabarti (1995). "Scope and Feasibility of Rabbit Farming" *Farmers and Parliament,* 30 (10) 10–11.

Takkar, OP. and Jagjit Kaur (1997). "Reproductive Management of Rabbit". *Indian Farmer,* 46 (12) March: 3 5–39.

Tripathi, R.S. (1997). "Production and Marketing of Angora Wool Products in Uttar Pradesh Hills". *The Bihar Journal of Agricultural Marketing,* 5 (2) April–June, 1997.

Tripathi, R.S. Chandra Dev and M.L. Sharma (1995). "Economics of Angora Rabbit Farming in Hills. *Indian Journal of Animal Sciences* 65(6): 678–683.

Thakur, J.S. (2001). "Effect of Environmental conditions on Rabbit Production". Technical Lectures on Rabbit Production for Subject Matter Workshop-cum-Serninar on Rabbit Farming. Sponsored by Directorate of Extension, Ministry of Agriculture, Government of India. Organized by

Directorate of Extension Education through Department of Animal Nutrition, College of Veterinary and Animal Sciences, CSK Himachal Pradesh Krishi Vishvavidyalaya, Palampur -176 062. September 6–13, 2001: 67–72.

Tommer, S.S., Tomer, A.S. Kushwaha, P.S., Gautam, D.S. and Verma, O.P. (1992). "Study of Cost Benefit Analysis of Summer *Mung* Cultivation under Different Levels of Phosphorus Mixture, Moisture Regimens and Seed Rates in Alluvial Soils of Chambal Command". *Agricultural Science Digest* 12 (4): 199–202.

Tomek, W. and Robinson, K. (1990). "Agricultural Product Prices". Cornell University Press, Ithaca (down loaded from internet).

Zimmerman, E. and Gekle, L.(1985). *A Compendium of Rabbit Production,* Published by Deutsche Gesellschaft fur Technische Zusammenarbeit (GTZ) Gmbh, Dag – Hammarskjold Weg 1+2, D 6236 Eschborn 1, Federal Republic Germany.

INDEX